Informal Teaching
in the
Open Classroom

INFORMAL TEACHING IN THE OPEN CLASSROOM

Virgil M. Howes

Macmillan Publishing Co., Inc.
New York
Collier Macmillan Publishers
London

Copyright © 1974, Virgil M. Howes
Printed in the United States of America

Macmillan Publishing Co., Inc.
866 Third Avenue, New York, New York 10022

Collier-Macmillan Canada, Ltd.

Library of Congress Cataloging in Publication Data

Howes, Virgil M.
    Informal teaching in the open classroom.

    Bibliography: p.
    1.   Open plan schools.   I.   Title.
LB1029.06H68   372.1'102   73-8353
ISBN 0-02-357330-9

Printing: 2 3 4 5 6   Year: 5 6 7 8 9

*To the teachers and pupils who work
so hard to make the open classroom a reality.*

Preface

Dramatic changes occur when school is thought of as a way of life rather than a series of programs somehow squeezed into a rigid, timetabled day.

The move from teaching and directing to learning and living leads to significant discoveries. The search is no longer "boxed in" by demands for performance of trivia. How unessential and even harmful to human development is so much of our present attachment to scores, grades, external objectivity, and "educational barking"! What takes on significance is the *process of educating young children,* the quality of the experience, and the value of human interaction. We cannot be satisfied with product alone. Mastering a trivial skill is far less important than the attitude engendered. What happens to the child as he learns should be of far greater concern than mere cognitive understanding. Getting to where we are going must be as good a process as where we end up.

The quality of every facet of the educative process must be of concern—a deep concern that we not give to our young the things we would not tolerate as adults nor the things that we suffered, hated, and dreaded as we experienced those "golden hours of school." It is sadistic as well as absurd to feel children can suffer through such educative experiences just because we did.

There isn't a facet of education that doesn't need to be

explored if we are to act on our overriding concern that school must be arranged for the "kind of living" it affords the child. Our training of people, our materials, buildings, playgrounds, organizational schemes, curriculum content, our teaching interactions are all suspect. School can be a good place to live and still promote learning fully. It's not a more costly enterprise. Rather it's a reordering of priorities.

This is what the open classroom is about—*good education*. It is not a package deal, a shiny innovation, nor must it become a fad. The open classroom offers children a quality of human living in their learning as they experience their surroundings, explore their world, and grow in power to feel, think, and act in independent, responsible ways. The school moves away from being an institution of "doing something to someone" to becoming a place for growing and developing. Resources are viewed not in terms of material things alone but in terms of ideas emerging from children, experiences shared by classmates, and everyday things provided close at hand. And teachers, as humans, facilitate, guide, and serve, thus replacing manipulation and domination. But to love is not enough. The teacher acts in positive ways to help the child bring to consciousness that which he is experiencing, to link learnings, and to turn activity into deeper meanings through analysis and interpretation.

The daily task of developing promising practices for the open classroom is an evolutionary process. Teachers and pupils alike learn that experimentation is crucial. *Let's try it and see how it works* becomes a basic attitude. The teacher, however, weighs and interprets results against ever sharper ideas of the direction toward which growth is desired. How do you create freedom and let responsible decision making grow? What is "good" in terms of the living-learning environment? How does the school become a positive support for growth rather than a directing force for training? What are the "learnings" that are developing? How does the teacher facilitate and intervene in positive ways?

This work attempts to construct steps that are a start toward informal teaching in the open classroom. Practical suggestions for development grow out of the theory, assumptions, and values underlying the open classroom. First steps as well as ways to analyze what is happening toward a fuller implementation are discussed.

Experienced teachers as well as students preparing to be teachers should find this book useful. There is common ground. Both are or will be working in school settings that predominantly reflect conventional practices. Both will be working with children who are predominantly used to conventional practices (except those children who are new to school) and who will need help in adjusting to a freer situation. And both will be working in a community and parent setting whose own school experience will largely reflect conventional practices.

Although the experienced teacher will have to overcome familiar patterns, there will be resources of "knowing I can work with children" and "feeling I want to change because I know from experience what I've been doing is not satisfying to me or to many children." These are powerful agents to assist in the process. The student now preparing to teach, though not having to change teaching patterns, needs specific guidance because a "set" or frame of reference has been built somewhat from his personal experiences of teachers operating in conventional ways.

Consideration of these factors and a recognition that the educated teacher is building upon much knowledge and understanding has influenced the content of the chapters to follow. Material related to child growth and development, children's learning, and specific knowledge in various disciplines is assumed to be already a part of the teacher's background. This professional understanding and knowledge will be continually added to by the teacher through study, reading, and experience. But it is not the focus for this volume. Rather implementation and practical application of this body of knowledge in a way to free the learner to become "his own best teacher" is the thrust of this work. How the working of the open classroom develops is the basis for the ideas and thoughts to follow. How the open classroom develops for an individual teacher depends on his experiences with his pupils as he translates the underlying premises and values into meaningful practices.

The author is deeply grateful to the many teachers in numerous schools who have contributed in so many ways to this work. At times it has been the sharply worded question that has forced the author to think in fresh ways about the practical application of some theoretical assumption or basic tenet. Others have shared successes that have become examples reported here. Still others have been generous in providing materials they have developed that may be a basis for a form or technique described. Principals and teachers have invited the author to photograph classroom scenes and happenings. Some of these are used to illustrate facets of the open classroom at work. The list could go on, for dedicated teachers developing exciting programs are eager and most willing to share. To name the many schools, the hundreds of teachers, and the many children who have talked to the author and contributed in some way would call for a never-ending list. Nevertheless, to each the author is most appreciative, and he hopes that this work will add useful dimensions for other teachers interested in exploring the open classroom concept.

V. M. H.

Acknowledgments

The author is deeply grateful to many individuals, teachers, administrators, and consultants who have shared so generously their joys, problems, and practical tips. Numerous schools could be named that have contributed generously in one form or another. Sometimes it was a practice, or a permission to photograph classroom scenes, or a sample record, or an opportunity to talk with children and view their work. Recognizing that some school may inadvertently be omitted, nevertheless the author wishes to recognize especially the generosity of the following schools and centers:

Almaden Elementary School
San Jose Unified School District, California

Bousfield Infants' School
Inner London Education Authority
England

Fairfield Primary School
Leicestershire Education Authority
England

Acknowledgments

       Grand View Elementary School
       Manhattan Beach City Schools, California

       Grape Street Elementary School
       Los Angeles Unified School District, California

       Halford Infants' School
       Inner London Education Authority
       England

       Ladbroke Mathematics Center
       Inner London Education Authority
       England

       Ohlones Elementary School
       Palo Alto Unified School District, California

       Palomar Elementary School
       Chula Vista City Schools, California

       Prior Weston Primary School
       Inner London Education Authority
       England

       Stebon Primary School
       Inner London Education Authority
       England

       Thurmaston Church Hill Infants' School
       Leicestershire Education Authority
       England

Contents

Contents

Informal Teaching
in the
Open Classroom

CHAPTER 1

The Open Classroom—
Good Education

Open education is a way of thinking about children, about learning, and about knowledge. It is characterized by openness, freedom with responsibility, and trust in children. The classroom is a good place to live as well as a good place to learn.

Descriptions of the open classroom in action highlight many attributes—activity, informality, children's involvement, expressive work, multi-age-grouping patterns, curriculum integration, heterogeneity, relevance to the child's world, and more. Such classrooms do indeed look, sound, and feel different from the typical conventional classroom attended by most of us and even taught in by most of us.

There are also, however, rumors and reports of chaos, noise, shallow work, idle pursuit of casual interests, "do your own thing." But these unsatisfactory results, if they exist, are errors of application that abridge the underlying tenets of open education. Chaos is no condition of effective learning. Nor is the open classroom chaotic. The casual observer may indeed see unfamiliar conditions but the classroom participants do know what is going on, what they're about, and where things are. Activity and involvement must not be misinterpreted as chaos. There is structure and organization in the functioning open classroom but it is centered with the participants, not the teacher alone in an authoritarian pattern.

Silence is neither "golden" nor necessarily conducive to

learning. But noise does not prevail when people are deeply involved in tasks meaningful to them. The open classroom is more frequently a place with "humming sounds" of learning because children are engaged in conversations, expressing sounds of discovery and insights, and interacting in natural ways as they ask and inquire. Stillness and silence need justification, but not talk and the hum of learning.

Children at play are children at work. Play as the exploration of a casual interest is frequently the start of a working together by the child with other children in the exploration of a problem. Play as the method of tackling a concern is a natural development as the child attempts to gain meaning about his world. Dimensions explored help to develop reality and new insights. But "doing your own thing," if this is what it is, does not mean being antisocial or shallow. There is disciplined planning. There is thinking about what to do, how to do it, and the desired outcome. The teacher is active and involved, lending guidance and support, bringing to the conscious level new insights, and challenging the pupils with new questions.

The open classroom is more than an *integrated day, integrated curriculum,* or *informal education.* These are terms describing only partial facets of the open classroom. The integrated day refers to situations in which learning is not divided into disciplines or subjects. Experience cuts across all areas. Subjects such as reading, math, and science are not the day's focus. Rather the learning, problem solving, or discovery engaged in by the child in relation to his needs and interests involves in a natural way components from many subjects. Certainly the integrated curriculum is one of the dimensions of the open classroom.

Likewise, informal education is a practice found in the open classroom. The attempt is to move away from the rigid timetable, the formally prescribed lessons and assignments, and the traditional "directing" role of the teacher. But informal methods are, again, only an aspect of the open classroom.

SOME BASIC TENETS

What then is the open classroom? It is both a good place to live and a good place to learn. It is neither an invention of the

British nor a sudden innovation. It is solidly rooted and has been evolving over a period of time.[1] It is good education, not a fixed model of practices or techniques, nor a neatly packaged program. It is built upon basic tenets that have characteristic practices and important supports. The teacher who wants to develop a meaningful program will do more than incorporate some of the elements into his daily work. More openness, more pupil choice, more teacher-pupil involvement, and activity in learning, as desirable as these attributes may be, *do not* make a fully functioning open classroom.

There are some basics to be followed. And although a classroom may incorporate many desirable practices, it is not functioning as open if these basics are being abridged. Such tenets are the bases for the development of practices and procedures. The teacher beginning to move toward developing the open classroom uses an understanding of the concepts to develop his pattern of implementation. He realizes fully that the first steps are along a path leading to a desirable destination. With this idea firmly in mind the teacher avoids falling in the trap of blaming the open classroom concept for difficulties encountered. He recognizes that it is the application that is in error and that needs modifying, rather than a failure of the open classroom tenets. An understanding of open classroom foundations such as these helps:

1. There is a basic *respect* for each child. His purposes, needs, interests, and wants are central. Providing experiences and opportunities, planning, helping, facilitating—all these facets support the growing, developing child. There is *trust* that the child wants to learn, is learning, and will learn. The learner-teacher relationship is built upon a strong belief in the *integrity of the individual.* The interaction is like that of

---

[1]For discussion of the mainstreams of the open classroom concept and the contributions of various theorists and psychologists, see such references as the following: (1) John Blackie, *Inside the Primary School* (New York: Schocken Books, 1971); (2) Lillian Weber, *The English Infant School and Informal Education* (Englewood Cliffs, N.J.: Prentice-Hall, Inc., 1971); (3) Charles H. Rathbone, ed., *Open Education: The Informal Classroom* (New York: Citation Press, 1971); (4) ASCD Yearbook Committee, *A New Look at Progressive Education* (Washington, D.C.: ASCD, 1972); (5) Molly Brearley and others from the Froebel Institute, *Fundamentals in the First School* (Oxford: Basil Blackwell, 1969), and Roland S. Barth, *Open Education and the American School* (New York: Agathon Press, 1972).

INFORMAL TEACHING IN THE OPEN CLASSROOM ·

a partnership, with each participant working, sharing, enjoying, and contributing to deepen the experience and involvement. The open classroom supports the natural growth of
the child as he seeks experiences and opportunities to widen
and expand his understanding, knowledge, and ability to
function in the world he lives in.

2. Each child is recognized as an individual. The wholeness of
his growth and development is understood. There is belief
and trust in the child as a curious, active, seeking being.[2]
These characterizations are intertwined and interrelated, not
separate and apart. Each is part of the other and basic to the
structure and functioning of the open classroom.

   Individual differences are well known, accepted as
truth, and well documented. As each child is born an

---

[2]See Lillian Weber, *The English Infant School and Informal Education*
(Englewood Cliffs, N.J.: Prentice-Hall, Inc., 1971), pp. 173-188, for a further
discussion of these characteristics.

individual, he develops as an individual in individual ways and all experiences are personal and individual in meaning. The task of schooling is to build from the foundation up upon a full recognition that the child, each child, is unique and individual. Considering individuality and uniqueness as basic building blocks is very different from building to foster or to encourage individuality. The individual's uniqueness of experience, his perceptions and understandings, and his interests are the school's starting points, from which to foster continued growth and development. These are the links to new experiences and extensions for further learning and patterning. This growth occurs in the child as a whole. There are differences in rates of intellectual, emotional, social, and physical development. Nevertheless all are intertwined within the whole. A child grows, develops, and responds as a total being, not as separate parts.

In the process of learning he is an active agent. He seeks opportunities and experiences to find out about his world.[3] He makes sense of that which he takes in through the assimilative, accommodative process.[4] Piaget regards these functions as our most fundamental processes of learning and growth. *Assimilation* refers to the process of absorbing and organizing experiences from the activities that produce them. *Accommodation* refers to the modification of the assimilation process because many situations or experiences resist the known pattern. The child tries them on, causing, in turn, some changes in the existing pattern. This important part of learning or intellectual growth is done by the child himself, through his actions as the agent for his own learning. The child, then, must have the support conditions that allow him to be an active learner and that use his own questions and directions as next steps for learning. Schooling processes must not get in the way. The child needs freedom to experiment. Opportunity for interaction within a rich

---

[3]Olson's work related to seeking and self-selection is of great importance. Note especially Willard C. Olson, "Seeking Self-Selection and Pacing in Use of Books by Children," *The Packet* (Boston: D. C. Heath and Company, Spring 1952).

[4]Piaget's work has contributed immeasurably to our understanding of how a child learns. Note especially the "Selected References" at the end of the book for a fuller understanding of Piaget's contributions.

environment supports and builds interests for continued interaction, affording assimilation and accommodation. The role of teaching is to facilitate, because direction must be the child's own role.

3. The organization, management, teaching, and interaction of classroom elements function on the basis of openness. It is an open system in terms of learning, conditions for learning, and human relationships. Ending points and learning outcomes emerge from the experience and the sense the child makes of it. Preconceived objectives imposed externally upon the learner are inappropriate. These and such an attribute as fixed knowledge to be learned by all are characteristics of a closed system.

   In an open system there are "starters" but the knowledge to result and the ideas to be explored expand and develop through the experience. The hierarchical role of the teacher is diminished. There is honesty and sensitivity to the individual. The relationship takes on the character of trust and belief in the worth of the individual. And the structure is that which promotes freedom rather than maintains control. There is flexibility and adaptability. New challenges and ideas are met in an honest, open way.

4. The power structure for learning is centered on the child. He grows in the feeling of self-power and control over his learning. The adult supports the child as he works toward being his own best teacher. Decisions and responsibility for actions are central to the child's schooling experience. He learns through active participation in decisions related to what is to be learned, how the task is to be undertaken, and the effects and results of the experiences. The child builds feelings of confidence, grows in thinking, and develops the ability to solve problems by being an active agent.

ESSENTIAL CHARACTERISTICS

These are ideas basic to the open classroom. They are very much interrelated and no doubt could be broken into many finer points. Other ideas could probably be added. And yet each encompasses numerous concepts and related ideas. This formulation of essential foundations can be further clarified by a look at characteristics that emerge as the open classroom takes on fuller meaning. Essential aspects include the following:

1. The curriculum moves away from being an *independent* variable to being a *dependent* variable. It becomes child centered. It is relevant to the child's needs, interests, curiosities, and purposes. The concept of essential knowledge takes on personal meaning rather than sameness for all. The classroom is filled with "starting points" but not expected coverage. Children are engaged in interdisciplinary activities.
2. The pupil has freedom to make real choices. Self-selection is recognized as a crucial form of human development. Children make learning decisions and significant choices, and they accept responsibility for the outcomes. Growth in self-direction is nurtured and supported.
3. How a child learns, the questions he asks, the way he solves problems, his thinking development are of prime importance. The process of learning is at least as important, if not more so, than the knowledge that is gained.
4. The teacher actively participates with the child as he engages in experiences of personal relevance. The hierarchical roles of teacher-director and learner-recipient are gone. The teacher supports, facilitates, guides, questions, connects, and brings to a conscious level learnings and insights of the child.
5. There is an atmosphere, human relationships, and conditions that allow a child to change, to reconsider perceptions, and to integrate new insights freely. There is no fear of losing face if one admits error or holds varying values and beliefs. The child is not defenseless. He is free, he is accepted, he can "bare his soul" without repressions, guilt, or loss of ego.
6. Skill learning grows out of the child's own work. Skills follow rather than precede experiences and activities that provide a base for understanding and concept development. Skills taught as a program divorced from the child's own learning not only results in rote learning but, more importantly, may block real understanding.
7. Children are free to explore an individual interest deeply. The work and flow of a child's day is viewed as individual. Balance in terms of learning is viewed over the long range.

The focus is on intellectual growth rather than the specific knowledge acquired.

8. Children collaborate with each other when interests are similar, when there are activities that demand group endeavors, when combining individual talents and learnings helps in the accomplishment of goals beyond the capabilities of an individual, or when working together yields meaningful results, joys, developments to the individuals concerned.

9. There is creative work. A wide range of resource materials is available for the child to use. The teacher helps the child explore new techniques, learn new ways of expressing himself. There is discussion, personal talk with the child about his explorations and work. Questions that help to bring out conscious understanding of learning or that may foster further exploration are asked. The child extends his range of creative work, which helps him make personal expressions about his world, tackle and solve real problems, and become increasingly discriminating in his response to experience.

IMPORTANT SUPPORTS

There are many attributes that support the open class-room. They are important features and conditions that help the open classroom to build on basic tenets. Nevertheless, these supports are not in themselves the essence of openness. Instead they may be first steps toward openness. They are beneficial improvements. And they are usable with many styles and strategies of instruction. The applicability of these supports does not detract from the importance but does mean that they should not be mistaken for the open classroom. If these alone are observed, with the previous tenets and characteristics missing, then there are only the trappings of openness.

Such supports are numerous. Some specific ones that are frequently found include the following:

1. The classroom environment is rich with materials, ideas to explore, and things to use. It offers diverse opportunities. Learning centers, work storage areas, exhibits, children's projects, and construction activities are available to stimulate interest and extend learnings.
2. Management procedures are flexible. Informal interactions are permitted and encouraged. There are class meetings and discussions relevant to problems and developments of the day.
3. The daily schedule is less rigid. There is a wholeness to the day. It flows smoothly rather than being chopped into tiny pieces and segments. Children are given broad latitude relative to the scheduling of their work pursuits.
4. Workshop methods, activity, and doing are evident. Assignments and lectures are minimal or nonexistent. Children are involved in concrete experiences. Manipulative experiences and activities are emphasized.
5. Children's ideas are expressed through the use of a variety of media and methods. There is much evidence of children's work projects, murals, recordings, writings, art, construction, models, and so on. The room reflects the fact that the children have individual pursuits and are active in learning.
6. Room arrangement may include different activity areas. There may be comfortable furniture (sofas, pillows, over-

stuffed chairs). Parts of the room or the whole room may be carpeted. Children may have boxes or cubbyholes rather than desks for the storage of personal learning materials. Tables may be more in use than individual desks. Bulletin boards may be filled with children's work; the arrangement may even look messy.

7. Children may keep individual records of plans, of studies, and of progress. There is increased responsibility for one's own learning.
8. The teacher holds individual conferences with each pupil about his learning, interests, expectations, and needs and about his questions.
9. There is a greater heterogeneity in age grouping. The teacher may have a class of children with ages spanning two, three, or more years.

   The open classroom is a fundamental redesigning of all

parts of the classroom. It is not another new technique, way of working, or arrangement of some elements. It evolves from philosophical and psychological foundations spanning numerous years and from the work of many theorists and practitioners. It is a *new school.*

GOALS, OUTCOMES, AND ADVANTAGES

The open classroom does not function without goals and beliefs relating to the rights pupils can expect from schooling. Based on these rights, dimensions of schooling and the pattern of practices take shape. The form of daily actions establishes the nurturing environment that supports children's growth.

The experience of schooling provides meaningful opportunities for children in

- The right to practice independence and responsibility.

- The right to greater freedom and self-direction.

- The right to a greater share in shaping the institution of which they are a part.

- The right to grow and develop in an atmosphere free from fear and manipulation, psychological and physical.

- The right to explore beliefs, values, and connections, as important, vital aspects of life.

- The right to be involved in the process of learning, not conditioned and manipulated to respond.

These rights help to shape the individual's feelings about himself and others. When fully implemented in the program, structure, and conduct of the open classroom, these rights also contribute to the attainment of the goals of open education:

- Children who know themselves as persons with limitations and strengths.

INFORMAL TEACHING IN THE OPEN CLASSROOM

- Children who think independently, act responsibly, and are self-propelled.

- Children who use time efficiently and effectively for their own learning and living purposes.

- Children who understand deeply democratic values and beliefs and apply them in daily life.

- Children who show a great concern for other children, valuing the opinions of others in the solution of problems.

- Children who like themselves and feel good about themselves.

- Children who use their environment and available resources well.

- Children who have healthy egos that are not dependent on or slaves to either the inner or the external worlds.

- Children who like school, want to go to school, and are happy in school.

- Children who make more and more learning decisions and accept responsibility for them.

- Children who have confidence in themselves and in their ability to confront and solve problems.

- Children who know how to learn, view learning as worthwhile, and think of learning as a lifelong process.[5]

The open classroom takes on substance from these goals. They serve as guides for the teacher's thinking as he works to develop a school setting and plans resource opportunities for

---

[5]Adopted and modified from a series of statement developed by Helen Darrow, Virgil Howes, Robert Keuscher, and Louise Tyler, January-March 1968.

children to experience and understand their world and their relationship to it.

The open classroom is the kind of good education a democratic society develops for its young citizens. Just learning is not enough. In a democratic society there are basic premises that must not be overlooked in the practice of schooling. There are foundations of values, beliefs, and attitudes that are essential building blocks. The means are important. These carry messages to the learner that mold and shape his learnings. Practices that are compatible with goals strengthen the quality of experience. To separate one from the other is to send a garbled communication to the learner as to what democracy is, can be, or should be.

CHARTING YOUR TRAVEL

With a base of understanding, a belief in the importance of the quality of educational experience basic to the open classroom, and a desire *to get on with it,* the teacher is ready to deal with application. There is no one way. It is a developing process. The teacher needs to set a firm direction of experiment and research. *Would this work? Is it consistent with the tenets of open education? What happens when it's tried? What changes are needed? What are the next steps?* These are questions for the teacher to pursue as he seeks to develop the open classroom. It is not gimmicks, or techniques, but practice built upon careful thought and experimentation that yields solid growth toward the desired goal.

The chapters that follow can help to open up possibilities. The material comes from personal experiences, talks with numerous teachers, questions and challenges from parents, work in helping schools to change, and the sharing of ideas by many colleagues in a variety of positions in the education world. There are ideas to build on, suggestions for thinking out next steps, analyses of situations and techniques to show components, examples and visual aids, references for further reading, and considerations to stretch thinking, deepen insights, and strengthen practices that the teacher develops himself. Here's

how one teacher viewed the need for change and the beginning
joys, discoveries, and commitments:

I thought I was an expert—a top-notch teacher, strong in relating academic skills to my children, firm in insisting that they implement the skills I had taught them, demanding their best and only their best efforts and accepting nothing but perfection. My standards were high. I was no slouch. I worked hard and demanded as much from my students.

What happened? After eight years of classroom teaching I was ready to walk out the door, walk away from the very profession I had chosen. I had turned the very thing that I once loved into a totally de-personalized experience. I had become so concerned with curriculum, with imparting skills and facts that when the children reacted to me as the free and spontaneous beings they should be, they are, I turned them off completely. Things were fine outside the classroom, away from school. There with children, I was me! Not Miss Bosco who should be, who *must* be teaching them something. Teaching had become a chore. Each day I hated it more.

Two of my co-workers sensed my feelings of dissatisfaction. One, in particular, invited me to take this course. I had little hope that anything would help my dilemma. One question I asked myself over and over again. I had chosen this profession wholeheartedly, idealistically, and enthusiastically, completely of my own accord.

I remembered a snowy winter in New York eight years past—my first teaching assignment—

"I can't believe I'm getting paid to do this. It doesn't seem like work at all." I had said those very words to a fellow teacher.

What *had* happened? The joy, the pleasure, the fun in *doing* had somehow been taken from me. In turn, I could impart none of the beauty and pleasure in learning to the children.

Very slowly, only since I have started this course and have found again that school can be and should be a place where children are themselves, where I am me, where we can act and react to each other, where we can meet and share and live a little together each day, am I beginning to see the direction in which after eight years I must and want to move.

We're having fun at school again! I know it's not going to be easy but that's what I *want* to do. And so, slowly and optimistically that old "Teacher" mold will be broken.

You see, again, I'm *motivated*, I *care* about what I'm doing. It's not all a chore any more. But, *I* have made these *choices* and along with them, I must accept and meet the responsibilities.

I can impart some of these feelings to my children—hopefully school will not be a PLACE of confinement within walls, within the pages of a book, or a follow-up.

Forgive me if I have not taken an intellectual approach in dealing with this. But you see, I, too, am just beginning to learn and to enjoy learning again.

—Angel Anne Bosco

You're invited to read along, to add your thoughts, and to begin
your personal travel along the trail of open education.

CHAPTER 2

The Living and Learning Environment for the Open Classroom

Opening the classroom door should be as exciting as opening a gift package. But a first step should not fully reveal what's inside. The environment for learning should be so enticing as to invite an extensive exploration. The many secrets, opportunities, and adventures possible should require a thorough examination of the contents inside.

The classroom environment must be a setting for personal learning rather than teaching. It is planned to invite discovery by action. It suggests experimentation and involvement. It demands individual attention and personal response. And it opens up vistas for expansion and exploration.

The classroom becomes a setting not only to raise questions but also to provide the tools and materials needed to answer questions emerging from personal experience and exploration. It is a stimulus for learning as well as a workshop-laboratory filled with useful aids. Nooks, crannies, and special learning areas along with individual work spaces and group areas are part of the total arrangement. Junk articles, throwaway items, printed material from books to clippings, and tools and equipment of all sorts make up the contents.

In the open classroom it is expected that children will see and handle materials, will move about the entire learning area, and will engage in all kinds of practical work and experiments. Curriculum is viewed in the context of possible journeys and emergent learnings rather than "coverage" and specified learnings. Materials are included with a basic premise that they may provide "starting points." The directions for explorations are many and individual. Consequently the environment is created to support the premise of "opening up" rather than "closing down." Teaching that is imposed and that includes predetermined ends is scrapped. The environment is built to support children's own thinking and deductions.

Creating and putting together the learning environment is a major teacher task. There is no one way, no standardized procedure. The environment is built from an understanding and knowledge of the children involved and the resources available and an understanding of children's learning.

There are a number of questions and concerns that are helpful to explore as the teacher formulates ideas for constructing the learning environment.

1. What are the children's interests? What tools and materials will support and extend their interests? What topics may be of interest?
2. What furniture and room arrangement will facilitate active learning? What equipment and storage arrangements can be devised? What work areas will be needed?
3. How can communication of learnings and sharing be supported and encouraged? What display space can be designed? How can walls, ceilings, and floor be utilized? What spaces outside the classroom can be used and how?
4. What provisions can be made for personal belongings and "brought-in" materials and objects? What will be needed as children move away from individual desks toward use of the total room?
5. What are children like in terms of physical needs for learning? They sprawl or lie on the floor to read or play games; they stand to write on a cabinet or shelf, and so on. What provisions should be made for the physical ways in which children learn and that they find natural for learning?

The teacher's first steps then may be to plan the physical environment of the classroom. One way is to draw the class-

THE LIVING AND LEARNING ENVIRONMENT FOR THE OPEN CLASSROOM

room to scale on a large sheet of graph paper. On separate sheets draw to scale each piece of movable furniture and cut them out. This makes it easy to try various classroom arrangements.

CLASSROOM LAYOUT GUIDELINES

Many teachers find it useful to think in terms of areas within the classroom for various activities. If a large space is shared by two or more teachers, or if there are closet space, hall areas, or other available space then these can be considered as the plan is developed. In the layout of areas there may be a general division of activities in terms of noisy and quiet as well as clean and messy. Four general sections can be arranged with attention given to the details noted in Figure 2-1.

FIGURE 2-1

QUIET/MESSY ACTIVITIES SECTION	NOISY/MESSY ACTIVITIES SECTION
Useful Special Features	Useful Special Features
Easily cleaned floor surface. Water/sink.	Outside exit. Open space to move around in easily. Easily cleaned floor surface.
Examples of types of areas	Examples of types of areas
Baking/cooking area. Art/paint/clay/junk area. Sewing/needlecraft area.	Wood construction area. Various project work area.
QUIET/CLEAN ACTIVITIES SECTION	NOISY/CLEAN ACTIVITIES SECTION
Useful Special Features	Useful Special Features
Good lighting for reading. Individual work areas.	Carpeted floor space. Special lighting.
Examples of types of areas	Examples of types of areas
Reading/library/research area. Math area. General work area.	Music area. Typing area. Dress-up/drama area. Home/play/house area.

INFORMAL TEACHING IN THE OPEN CLASSROOM

Other possibilities to consider in developing the general layout include these.

- Bookcases, cabinets, and similar furniture can serve as dividers if placed at right angles to walls rather than flat against the wall. The backs can be used to display children's work.

- Individual desks for each pupil are not needed. Seating accommodations can include ordinary chairs, sofas or couches, benches, stools, soft chairs, rugs, cushions, and boxes.

- Working surfaces should be varied. With a flexible program not all children will need the same type of surface at the same time. Some will need large tables, some individual spaces, others may be using the floor, working at easels, or sitting on the sofa. When the class comes together, they can use cushions, carpeting, mats, chairs, and so on, or sit on the floor.

- Individual pupil storage space can be plastic tray bins, shoeboxes, ice-cream barrels (check at your local ice-cream shop for empty five-gallon barrels) shoe boxes (frequently available in quantity from the shoe store), or cardboard boxes from the grocery store. Each pupil can decorate his own container, which is then stacked in a bookcase or bound together with others with masking tape (the ice-cream barrels can also be stacked horizontally to form a pyramid).

- Room dividers can be cardboard attached to the back of a work top or cupboard, peg board hinged together in three panels, corrugated cardboard used around selected pieces of furniture to designate work areas, or bookcases and cupboards set out in the room.

- Individual study areas can be devised in the storage closets found in some rooms. Such closets may be six or seven feet tall with double doors. If the doors are kept open into the room at right angles to the wall (the doors can be tied together or held by floor stops), natural divisions are provided. Inside the closet a shelf can be added at work height. If shelves are already there, one may have to be removed to allow sufficient space. With a chair, individual cubicles are available and yet little storage space is lost.

- A sheet of vinyl can be laid down over floors or carpeted areas to protect against spills during messy activities. The vinyl is easy to clean and can be rolled up after use.

- Cupboards and cabinets are often easier to use without doors. The doors can be used as table tops or room dividers, used on the floor to provide flat surfaces, or hinged to the wall to make additional display or work space depending on how they're attached.

- Panels of colored burlap can serve as dividers as well as exhibit areas for the children's work.

The next step is to decide what to include in the learning

THE LIVING AND LEARNING ENVIRONMENT FOR THE OPEN CLASSROOM

environment. The current interests of the children, the available materials and resources, and the teacher's ideas for adding to and expanding the children's work are all factors to consider. These ideas can generally be organized into two major groupings:

1. General work areas that relate to the storage of materials and equipment grouped around some general theme—*theme-work areas.*

INFORMAL TEACHING IN THE OPEN CLASSROOM

2. Specific investigative centers developed as "starters" that propose possible things to test out, study, or research—*investigative learning centers.*

In each of these types there are numerous useful possibilities.

STORAGE AND THEME-WORK AREAS

Definite places are needed for the storage of the many materials, tools, equipment, and apparatus found in the open classroom. Frequently these items can be grouped in meaningful ways for storage. Combining appropriate work space with the effective storage of related items can create an activity area that relates to some overall theme or general work interests.

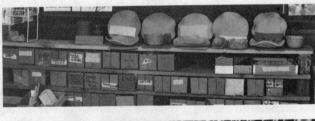

The teacher may add starter ideas, activities, or experiments to try in a specific work area. Ideas of "what to do" may help children begin exploring the materials found in the area. Later they may branch out into more independent work directions and not need such help. It must be remembered that such areas are intended to be basically open. There is no intent to direct the child's activity or to expect the coverage of certain material. Basically the setup is to help the children know where various materials and equipment can be found. There is, of course, freedom for the child to use the materials in ways other than the general theme or work interest suggested.

The areas to include at any one time will vary from room to room. The physical size of the room will determine the number. Changing interests will affect the kinds of work areas and the specific activities. Although some of the material and equipment will be permanent, how they are organized, stored, and combined with work space will change. New items within a work area or even new starter suggestions by the teacher can influence the activity and work of the children.

A description of some of the storage and theme areas follows.

Reading/Library/Research Area

A carpeted area furnished with a comfortable sofa, an overstuffed chair, and cushions is useful. One or two tables at the side for individual study and writing may be needed.

Books should be displayed with front covers exposed. They will be much more apt to be picked up and used than those shelved with only the bound edge showing. The spine of a book is neither particularly attractive nor appealing.

Materials to have on hand include

- Library books covering a wide range of ability and interests.

- Newspapers, magazines, weekly readers.

- Catalogues, telephone directories, manuals for operating classroom equipment.

INFORMAL TEACHING IN THE OPEN CLASSROOM

THE LIVING AND LEARNING ENVIRONMENT FOR THE OPEN CLASSROOM

- Reference works—encyclopedias, dictionaries, atlases, maps.

- Paperback books, how-to-do-it books.

- Picture collections.

- Work games and other material that children may use to practice language skills, enlarge vocabulary, make progress in reading.

Listening/Viewing/Recording Area

Audio-visual materials should be as available to children as books and other reading matter. Such materials are additional resources to be used individually as well as by groups.

Teachers may offer instructional sessions on how to use various kinds of equipment, awarding certificates to children who successfully complete the program. Certificate holders can then use equipment at will and serve as aides on call by other children not yet qualified.

Egg cartons stapled over wall or divider surfaces can help with the noise problem. Large cubicles entirely covered with egg cartons can serve as recording areas. A cave made from material hung from the ceiling can darken an area useful for showing films and slides.

The area might include the following items:

- Cameras.

- Viewlex, graphlex, mini-loop.

- Overhead projector and transparencies.

- Listening post with earphones.

- Record player, records, tape recorder, tapes, microphone.

- Film projector, films (a catalogue may be made available so that children can do the ordering of the weekly supply from the school district or county center).

- Slide projector, slides, individual viewers.

- Screen (white cardboard or tag board can be used).

- Direction charts on how to use equipment.

Music Area

The music area should be freely available for the children not only to experiment with instruments but to develop musical interpretations of the world around them. A carpeted area and even carpets hung from the ceiling can help to soften the noise. Large cardboard boxes covered inside with egg cartons can serve as individual studios and help muffle the noise.

Possible materials to include in the area are

- All types of musical instruments—bells, castanets, chime-bars, cymbals, zither, triangles, xylophone, drums, ukulele, guitar, glockenspiel, and so on.

- Piano, organ (if possible).

- Instruments from olden days and other countries.

- Ideas on how to make instruments.

- Music boxes and records.

- Music books, sheets of easy-to-play music.

- Ideas on how to write music; blank music paper.

- Charts, pictures, and exhibits dealing with the development of music, instruments, and so on.

THE LIVING AND LEARNING ENVIRONMENT FOR THE OPEN CLASSROOM

Art/Paint/Clay/Junk Area

A variety of materials can be stored here not only for use in artistic expression but also for use in numerous experiments, project work, displays and exhibits, and individual investigations. Storage bins can be made from shoe boxes, plastic trays, or empty ice-cream containers. Although an attempt should be made to organize and separate items in some way, the teacher can expect to have the children occasionally re-sort items. Nevertheless, numerous containers stored on shelves easily accessible to the children can help to keep classroom clutter

INFORMAL TEACHING IN THE OPEN CLASSROOM

within liveable limits. In this area some of the materials to include would be as follows:

- All kinds of papers for drawing, painting, cutouts, and so on.

- Painting shirts.

- Easels, paints, brushes, crayons.

- Area to dry art work (e.g., a rope strung up with

clothespins, a wooden folding laundry rack, a rack that can be pulled up to the ceiling).

- Day table, large work tables.

- Kiln (this should probably be located in an area where children aren't apt to run or bump into it).

- Junk, everyday rubbish discards (send home a letter asking parents to save materials; children are to bring them in periodically on "junk day." Each child or a designated group sorts the material into appropriate boxes and containers). Useful items include scraps of material, small boxes, wire nails, bottle caps, rolls from paper towels or toilet tissue, aluminum pie tins, bits of candles, buttons, plastic bottles and jugs, egg cartons, screws, drinking straws, pieces of leather and felt, old keys, any broken appliance, spools, pine cones, old eating utensils, pots and pans, tin lids, beads, yarn, ribbon, coffee cans, magazines, wallpaper scraps, baby food jars, TV dinner trays, plastic bags, and so on.

- Shelves for storage (concrete blocks with boards on top stacked no higher than three blocks can be used).

Dress-Up/Drama Area

This area, well-supplied and developed, can be as useful for the older child as for the younger. Playing out helps children

INFORMAL TEACHING IN THE OPEN CLASSROOM

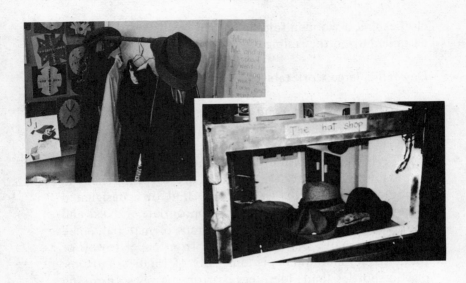

develop understandings of ideas, relationships, feelings, and attitudes. Creating and producing through drama is another form of communication, whether it be verbal or through movement. This area can include numerous props:

- Old costumes, clothes, coats, hats, ties, jewelry.

- Handbags, suitcases, wallets, shaving kits, trunks.

- Shoes, belts, scarves, umbrellas, gloves, fans.

- Aprons, uniforms (doctor, nurse, fireman, sailor, and so on).

- Mirrors, boxes to form a platform, miniature stage, spotlights.

- Puppet theater, finger socks and hand puppets, dolls, flannel board, flannel cutouts, stuffed animals.

Living Things—Plants and Animals Area

Growth, changes, care, and more take on deeper meaning in a "living things" area. Observation yields both data and questions as children work in the area. What to include is almost limitless. Some school districts have resources for teachers to check out animals, complete with cages, to the children for specified periods of time. Planting seeds, of course, is an easy way to start a collection of plants. And the children can contribute all sorts of things—from worms and snakes to frogs and cats. Terrariums, aviaries, and aquariums add other dimensions. Pictures, skulls, other bones, and preserved specimens might also be included.

Home/Play-House Area

Dividers, curtains, and cardboard can all be used to help partition off a space and create a setting. Furnishings and supplies are numerous:

• Cupboards, sink units, chairs, stools, refrigerator and stove (perhaps from cardboard), ironing board.

INFORMAL TEACHING IN THE OPEN CLASSROOM

- Toasters, coffee pots, irons, mixers (maybe old broken appliances).

- Pots, pans, dishes, knives and forks (plastic), glasses, bowls, molds, and cookie cutters.

- Equipment and supplies related to sweeping, polishing, dusting, washing, and scrubbing.

- Towels, aprons, chef's hat, dish rags.

- Boxes, tins, and other containers emptied of contents, but also real containers of grocery supplies.

- Recipes, measuring spoons and cups, scales, and timers.

- Pictures to hang, artificial flowers, vases, and odds and ends.

Wood Construction Area

A cart and cabinet or a rolling unit might contain basic tools:

- Hammers, saws, screwdrivers, drill, files, plane, sandpaper, vise, pliers, twist drills, metal saw, coping saw, square, straight edge.

A box or two for storage of materials and miscellaneous supplies might have the following:

- Pieces of wood, bamboo pieces, balsa wood, dowels, peg board, styrofoam, pieces of garden hose.

- Glue, nails, hinges, screws, wire, brads, rope.

- Cardboard of varying sizes and thicknesses.

- Cans (for wheels), spools, wheels from broken toys.

- Construction booklets, pictures of things to make.

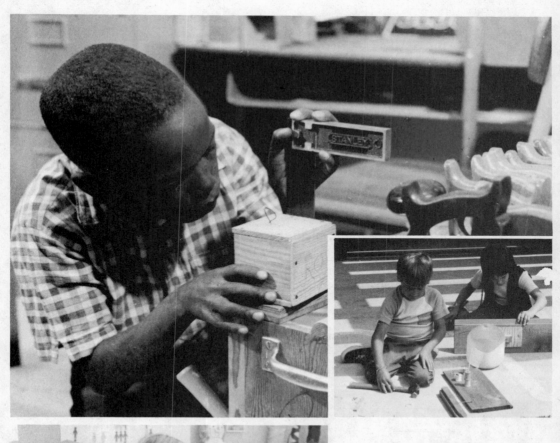

INFORMAL TEACHING IN THE OPEN CLASSROOM

Math Area

This working laboratory can be filled with tools and equipment related to numbers, shapes, quantities, sizes, measurements, weights, and so on. A partial listing of items to include follows:

- Assorted paper—graph, plain, large sheets, colored; pencils and pens, chalk.

- Machines such as adding machines, calculators, cash registers.

- Calipers (inside and outside), micrometer.

- Rulers, yardsticks, string, rope, rods, click wheel.

- Chain, string, rope, wire, tape measure.

- Containers of all sizes, measuring spoons.

- Clocks, candles, timers, egg timer.

- All kinds of games, puzzles.

- Spring scales, balances, kitchen scales with weights.

- Play money.

- Thermometer.

- Dienes blocks, attribute blocks, cuisenaire rods, dominoes, geoboards, geometric shapes.

- Protractor, compass.

- Lots of objects in containers, e.g., beans, seeds of all kinds, cones, paper clips, marbles, bottle caps, nuts, shells, corks, pebbles, nuts and bolts, nails, washers, clothespins, sugar cubes, dog biscuits.

- Fish weights (these come in various weights, so an assortment can be turned into scales).

- Activity cards, reference books, task cards, kits.

There are several other possible areas. Some need little space, perhaps only a corner or a small table. Others may require space that can be provided in a corridor, outside, or in a nearby building. Still others may be incorporated within the room or developed to replace an area that is seldom used. How working space and storage of items are grouped can vary extensively. Additional areas such as the following might be developed.

- Baking/cooking.

- Sewing/needlecraft.

- Water.

- Communications lab.

- Typing.

- Science.

- Social studies station.

- Building-block center (including large toys).

- Exploring area.

- Garden area.

Children working in an area may develop ideas to change the area or to create new ones. Some examples that have been developed include the following:

Radio Station.   A visit to the radio station by some of the girls with their Girl Scout troop was the beginning of a classroom radio station. Using some of the equipment from the listening/recording/viewing work area along with other materials that were brought in, the group set up a radio station, named MCLOA—the first initials of the girls who originally started it. Building on the interest, the teacher added resources and suggestions as to how it might function. Roles were decided upon—technicians, programmers, sponsors, news broadcasters, master of ceremonies, and so on. Programs were written for broadcasting. At first broadcasts were made in the room. Eventually the station was hooked up with the school's system and schoolwide broadcasts were made periodically.

Space Center.   The moon shots interested two boys. They began to construct cardboard models and collect written material about space and man's exploration. Soon an exhibit board was developed. One of the boys had a friend whose father worked in a space-connected industry. From the plant, the father obtained bits of material (defective parts) to give to the center. Other children became interested and joined the project. With the use of a cardboard box, a planetary system was constructed. Each planet was made to scale and all were hung by string in proper relationship to each other. Letters written to congressmen resulted in a variety of visual material and government pamphlets for the center. Slides were obtained from the school's audio-visual center. Some of the children prepared talks about their space center and what the scientists have found out. Before long the group became the school's experts and conducted scheduled visits to their space center and illustrated talks to other pupils in the school.

Post Office.   Some six- and seven-year-olds became interested in developing a post office. A visit by the class as well as a talk by a postman had spurred them to action. The post office was constructed from some of the large blocks, pieces of lumber, and various crates and boxes. There was a window to buy stamps and send letters and a window for parcels, furnished with a scale. Children began to bring in used postage stamps but eventually decided to make their own. Designs were created. The final choice was made by a group of children who acted as the postal committee. In order to have a variety, it was decided to issue commemorative stamps once a week. And of course various denominations had to be available.

A potato cut with zigzag lines and dipped in poster paint was used to cancel stamps. Mail had to be sorted and deliverymen were needed. Each of these problems was worked out so the post office became a functioning model.

Children were spurred on to writing letters and making things to mail as gifts. Soon letters and gifts for others outside the class began to appear. A whole new set of problems had to be solved—the establishment of post boxes in other places, schedules for delivery, pickup times to collect mail from boxes, and so on. The class post office became the post office for several rooms.

Museum.   Some articles from Mexico brought in by one pupil to share with the class resulted in a great deal of interest. Other pupils too had unusual items. A collection was started. The teacher brought in a collection of books. An exhibit was suggested; another child thought a museum would be better. Next to the teacher's lounge there was a small room that was vacant and contained just a few odds and ends. It was cleared, with permission from the principal, and the children began to brighten it up with paint, hanging materials, and even some odds and ends of wallpaper. Concrete blocks and boards were used for display stands. The children made dioramas of Mexican scenes they found in books. Notices were sent out asking other classes to collect articles for the museum. The class planned, organized, and created the museum. An official opening was planned with invitations sent to various school officials and parents. A booklet describing the museum contents was dittoed. Class members served as guides during museum hours. Students from the entire school could sign up for a visit. Special programs were developed by various groups and scheduled in connection with the museum. When interest in the Mexico exhibit ebbed the principal offered the museum space to others for their special interests.

Shopping Plaza.   In one class several children had developed a grocery store. They used empty food cartons to stock their shelves. They made price signs using newspaper ads. The check-out stand was equipped with a play cash register and play money. Other children wanted to start other stores, but space was a problem. After a talk with the principal, it was agreed that the auditorium could be used as long as stores were kept along the sides. With this help store construction began in earnest. Children working in pairs and small groups began to talk about the store they wanted to start. A master list was kept on the wall so that everyone would know what stores were being developed. Some children wanted to make sure their shop was the only one of a kind. Others seemed to want to make the same kind as some other group. The list grew—hat shop, grocery stores (two), shoe shop, pots and pans store, hobby store, bakery, dime store, jewelry store, department store, pet shop, candy shop, toy stores (two), and so on.

Each group was given a large box in which to collect items for their store. Signs, posters, even special shopping bags were made. Some children from other classes got interested and asked their teachers if they could make stores. Finally the teachers decided that the auditorium could be turned into a shopping plaza with each class developing stores. Each store group got the "stock" together first. Then the store would be set up in the auditorium. Eventually the plaza contained twenty-two different stores plus a sidewalk café, a medical clinic, a bank, and an optometrist's office. A directory map was made. Sales were held and children from all over the school would come to browse and shop.

THE LIVING AND LEARNING ENVIRONMENT FOR THE OPEN CLASSROOM

Other Examples. Numerous other project examples could be described. Some exhibits or work area centers are small and are created by one child. Others can be the result of large projects involving many children and lots of space. However, the common thread is that all come about because of a child's interest, idea, or contribution. The classroom environment with its varied and rich assortment of materials that the children see, handle, and use for their own creations definitely contributes to the process. Invariably other materials may be needed, but frequently the "starter" may be some material, equipment, or apparatus already in the classroom. A listing of some other centers developed by children follows. It shows what an enriching place the classroom can be when children are free to explore and develop.

INFORMAL TEACHING IN THE OPEN CLASSROOM

- TV station.

- Poetry corner.

- Art gallery.

- Hotel.

- Zoo (large papier-mâché animals).

- Observatory.

- Travel bureau.

- Home center (models of homes from various countries).

- Old western ghost town.

- Airport.

- Golf course (miniature).

- "Holiday Land" (celebrations and festivals representing holidays around the world—areas for each holiday created large enough for children to use).

- Newspaper office.

- Mortuary.

- Agricultural center.

- Lizard habitat area.

- Weather station.

- Sawmill.

- Water erosion model.

- Castle.

THE LIVING AND LEARNING ENVIRONMENT FOR THE OPEN CLASSROOM

- Telegraph station.

- Amusement park.

- Indian village.

- Fort.

- Train station.

When children are involved in creating, constructing, or developing a center, model, or work area there is integration of subject matter. Learnings are built as the child proceeds. There is continual use of reading, writing, and arithmetic. These are not studied in the abstract but take on meaning in relation to an interest and a need. In these situations solutions and learnings become effective and lasting. But even more is learned. Thinking is developed, how to work with others is stressed and ways to solve problems become evident. Experiencing results in learning, which builds foundations for the development of understanding.

INVESTIGATIVE LEARNING CENTERS

Specific centers developed in the classroom can be of help to many children. Some centers can be designed to provide starting ideas for exploring a particular topic. Other centers may provide direct help for tackling a learning difficulty the child wants to master. Still others can provide a focus for independent study of a particular subject or in a general area.

The investigative learning center differs from the theme-work area in that there are beginning directions, instructions, and guidelines on what to do and how to do it. The center is organized around a topic, a concept, a skill, or a specific problem. The working materials needed are usually available at the center or nearby. A beginning is directed through a specified task or question and some kind of recording is generally suggested. But, as in the theme-work area, there is no requirement that the centers be "covered" or used. They are available as resources to be used as wished as the child develops his overall working plan.

Many investigative learning centers are developed in connection with theme-work areas. The center with a related concern becomes part of the work area where the appropriate materials, equipment, and apparatus are stored. Because the center is specific, the work area may have two or three such centers at any one time. Frequent change of centers helps to keep interests alive and children productively engaged.

Centers are particularly useful for giving children ideas of what to do. When changes are made from conventional practices to more open practices children frequently find it difficult to take hold and become involved for any period of time. But carefully developed centers can help the children make useful plans and gain experience in a different way of working.

The intent of the investigative learning center is to promote individual and independent learning activities. The center, whether designed for an individual or for two or three children as a group, should be created and organized in such a way that spin-off activities are encouraged. The written task or set of directions, although starting in some specific way, should have an ending statement or suggestion that allows the child to move in a personal, individual way. In effect, there is no specific ending task but rather a spur to keep the job open and to move further along as the child himself determines. "I've finished that" should mean that the child has decided to end it rather than there being a specific ending because of the center itself.

Developing the investigative learning center requires that the teacher select a focus—a concept or topic from a discipline such as social studies, an interesting question to pursue, a possible experiment to conduct, a means of learning a skill, or a happening that may be of interest.

The next step is to write some kind of starter directions— to outline what is to be done. In order to avoid the trap of developing a center that demands a predetermined end, it helps to select the focus, then to think about the variety of learnings that could result. Then, rather than select any specific learning the teacher should try to write beginning directions in a way that enables the child to pursue the task and arrive at a learning most meaningful to him. The learning he develops may be any one of the possibilities thought of by the teacher or may even

THE LIVING AND LEARNING ENVIRONMENT FOR THE OPEN CLASSROOM

be something completely different. The investigative learning center, although focused on key ideas, need not be restrictive in terms of end learnings. The nature of these and the depth involved is personal and unique for the individual at his point of growth.

Developing centers that provide more than busy work or questions to answer requires thought. Establishing a focus and getting materials are easy steps. Putting the center together and writing good starter directions are the key elements. Some guidelines may help:

1. Set up the center to capture attention. For example, an interesting object or piece of equipment or an attractive design or picture might be the focal point. "What to do" cards or posters should be placed for easy reading. (Signs and direction charts hung from ceilings may be of interest to adults but the height is not conducive to easy reading by children, nor are words that attractive. Why should neck muscles be strained in finding out what might be done?)

2. Organize the materials so they can be kept orderly. Provide boxes to hold small items. Use a large box as the center with all materials and starter directions included. Fasten easy-to-scatter items to the table or hook them together in some way. Either include needed work space at the center or develop the center in such a way that it can be easily transported to an available and suitable work place.

3. Include a variety of starter idea cards for each center. (It's better to keep a card simple than to make it so complex that a child feels he doesn't want to do all those things.) A chart of ideas hung up tends to be boring to children after a day or two. Cards to be riffled through and chosen can at least get the child involved to some extent.

4. Write clear starter direction cards or charts:
   a. Use action statements as beginnings whenever possible—
      —"Find as many ways . . ."
      —"Observe carefully what happens when you . . ."
      —"Cut pictures from magazines to . . ."
      —"Take two (objects) . . ."
   b. Make explanatory statements when needed to clarify—
      —The focus.
      —A particular word.

      —A technique or process.

      —A specific step ("hint: start with the longest piece first").

  c. Provide examples in directions when needed, for instance, an example of how data is to be recorded or an illustration of a possible way to summarize.

  d. Conclude starter directions, whenever possible, with statements or questions that make the learning personal and that keep the activity open or invite the learner to move in a direction of his choice.

      —"What were your results . . . ?"

      —"What did you observe . . .?"

      —"What statements can you make . . . ?"

      —"What do you think would happen if you . . . ? Try it and see . . ."

      —"See if you can do . . . another way."

      —"What else might you do?"

      —"Ask five friends to (do this or answer your question or . . .). Compare the results."

      —"Compare your findings with . . . .What can you say now?"

      —"Show your results in another way (graph, chart, mural, art, music . . ."

A well-developed center can be geared for individual use, for a group working together, or for several individuals working in the center at the same time but by themselves. It is, however, generally intended that the center be able to be explored independently rather than under teacher guidance or supervision. But here a word of caution should be noted. The teacher should not assume that teaching must precede the use of a center. A center can be tried even if the child can't do what the teacher thought might be done. The child may develop something that has meaning to him. He may lose interest and leave it. Or he may start, get stuck, and need help at that point. Help can be available from another child as well as the teacher. Centers, then, are created for expanding as well as deepening experiences. Even technical vocabulary does not always need explanation in advance. Surprisingly, the child may know it, he may look it up, or at that point he may come and ask, "What does this mean?" Just because something has not been "covered" is no reason to assume that advance explanation is necessary.

Centers have many characteristics and functions, as have been described. The appropriateness more than anything else depends on the children who are involved. Their interests and needs are the factors to consider when the teacher is deciding which centers to develop. The level of difficulty of any center can be adapted, making it suitable for the young child as well as the older one. There is an almost inexhaustible variety of topics around which centers can be developed. Some possible topics, experiments, ideas, and concepts include the following.

Motors. How motors work; what they're used for; different types of motors; building motors run by wind or steam or electricity.

Time. All about clocks; what a child can do in various lengths of time; making clocks from water or sand or candles.

Collections. Developing collections, e.g., rocks, insects, leaves, foreign coins or stamps; collections built around colors or shapes.

Sense of Touch. Box of various objects to describe by touch; making "touch" collections; developing a touch exhibit, mural, or collage.

Sounds. Things that make various sounds; how sounds affect people; music sounds; experimenting with sound in water; how sound travels; making instruments and apparatus to carry sounds.

Electricity. Experimenting with batteries, bulbs, and switches; making simple electric motors, magnets, and so on; using electricity; developing electrical games and scoreboards; extent of electrical power, its effect on various areas (or countries).

Pets and People. Live animals and how they grow and eat, their habits, sleep patterns, movement or activity level, intelligence (e.g., learning a trick or following a maze); favorite pets; famous people and their pets; typical pets of various countries.

Capacity. Relationship of shapes to quantity; testing out quantities of various containers; developing problems related to capacity; investigating how capacity is used in medicine, cooking, building swimming pools; amount of water in oceans or lakes.

INFORMAL TEACHING IN THE OPEN CLASSROOM

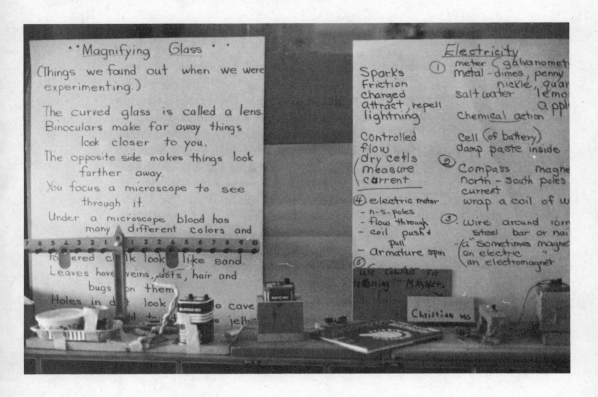

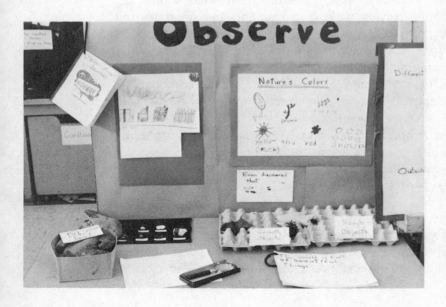

THE LIVING AND LEARNING ENVIRONMENT FOR THE OPEN CLASSROOM

Measuring. Using various instruments, e.g., tape measures, click wheels, rulers, yardsticks, rods, string, and so on; comparing measures made by different instruments; developing a list of measurements; measuring with other than standard measures, e.g., hands, noses, feet.

Throwing (Jumping, Running, Skipping, Hopping). Testing throwing power of individuals; making throwing machines; throwing and sports; throwing games; throwing power and relationship to size.

Making Maps. How to make maps; symbols of maps; mapping the school area, the home area, the neighborhood; developing scales; using road maps; pirate maps and treasure hunts.

Shadows. Shadow puppetry; using shadows to make shapes; insect life in shadow areas; effect of shadows on plants; telling time by shadows (shadow clocks); effect of shadow on temperature.

When we had weighed our dolls with batteries we measured them with batteries to see how long they were and then we measured ourselves with the same batteries.

INFORMAL TEACHING IN THE OPEN CLASSROOM

Tools. Flint arrowheads; tools of early man; making hand tools from stone; kinds of tools; tools versus machines; tool classification; surveys to find common tools; extent of use during stated periods, and so on; drawings, poems, related music.

Growing Plants. Seeds, their size in relation to the size of the plant; conditions for growing; experiments with plantings in various soils; effect of sound, wind, and so on, on plants; making books of plants; classifying plants; plants around the world.

Snakes and Lizards (Tadpoles, Frogs, Caterpillars, Butterflies, Mealworms, Grasshoppers). How they grow; their behavior; typical habitat; how they move; their speed in movement; diet; reactions to cold, dampness, light, warmth, sound, cramped quarters; where found in the world; numbers.

Small Animals, Birds, Fish. Mice, rats, hamsters, guinea pigs, chickens, gerbils, squirrels, birds, fish of all kinds, turtles—all can be used as focal points of specific centers or grouped around various ideas of diet, movement, growth, life span, locations where found, characteristics, and so on.

Motion or Movement. Experiments with pendulums; making sand patterns with pendulum swings; pendulum swings and time; uses of pendulums.

Temperature (Weather). Measuring temperature; temperatures at different times; using temperature to predict weather; temperatures around the world; temperature and plant growth.

Study of Trees. Different kinds of bark, leaf patterns, growth rate, and other characteristics; where found; diseases; weights of woods, uses; petrified wood; poetry and literature related to trees; legends and myths.

Making Movies Without Cameras. (Done with colored marking pens and 16mm blank film—similar to leader film; this can be obtained cheaply from a photography store.) Direction cards on how to make a film; using cassette player to add sound; developing animated characters; experimenting with colors, print, lines, shapes; use of self-stick paper on film; studying people's reactions to various films; investigating moviemaking with a camera.

Sources of More Ideas. There is an endless list of challenging and worthwhile ideas around which centers can be developed. A review of key concepts, understandings, skills, and

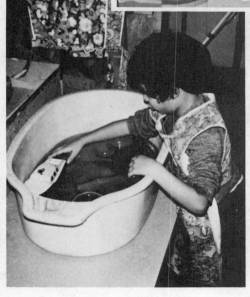

knowledge found in textbooks, teacher guides, courses of study, and general printed materials can help the teacher build ideas for centers. The teacher might find it useful to make a list of possible focal points for centers similar to those suggested. From time to time ideas can be added, and at the point when new centers are needed the teacher has a ready reference to review.

INFORMAL TEACHING IN THE OPEN CLASSROOM

Putting together a center requires some thought. Material must be gathered, "starter ideas" developed and things organized to stimulate interest. Examples of centers described in greater detail may help not only to clarify various discussion points but to provide useful ideas for adaptation and implementation.

"Our World of Smells"

Using a number of discarded baby food jars stuffed with cotton, the teacher made a smell center. Each jar's cotton was soaked in a different liquid or wrapped around a strong-smelling substance. Some of the things used were perfume, dishwashing liquid, vinegar, syrup, shaving lotion, rubbing alcohol, a piece of strong cheese, liquid floor cleaner, furniture polish, coffee grounds, moth balls, lemon juice, soy sauce, steak sauce, and mustard.

Each jar was numbered (a piece of paper with the number was put inside the jar facing out) and all jars were put together in an upright position in a large box. This box was cut with two sides sloping to the front, which was about 2 inches high. The back of the box was used for labeling—"Our World of Smells and You." Starter idea work cards (5 x 8 index cards) were placed in a plastic sleeve bag on the tall side of the box just below the label. A couple of these cards read as follows:

Card 3

Smell each bottle. Make a chart to show how you would classify each smell. (Write the number of the smell in the column that describes it best.) Your chart might have columns labeled:

Good Smells
"Okay" Smells
Unpleasant Smells

Make some statements about your findings.

Ask two friends to make a similar chart of their thoughts about the smells. Compare the findings. What can you say about the ways smells affect people? You might repeat this experiment with other friends and see what happens.

Card 5

Pick out any five bottles from the smell box. Smell one bottle and write down all the things it makes you think about. Smell the second bottle and write down all the things it makes you think about. Do the same for bottles 3, 4, and 5. What statements can you make about your results? You might ask some friends to try this and then make a big chart on "Smells and the Things We Associate with Them."

INFORMAL TEACHING IN THE OPEN CLASSROOM

"Junk Center"

A shoe box is filled with all sorts of junk—keys, rocks, plastic bits, wire, used stamps, spools, nails, tree bark, empty tubes, small boxes, paper clips, erasers, and all kinds of odds and ends. A caption on the top of the box reads, "What Can You Find Out?" Idea cards are in a pocket attached to the box. Some cards suggest taking several items and using their shape as a basis for a drawing and story or using them in some kind of a "make-believe" machine that is described in terms of how it works and what it does. Other cards suggest measuring, balancing, or weighing activities using objects singly or grouped in various ways. One card reads like this:

Card 6

Write a rule that allows you to sort all of the objects into exactly two piles. Then sort them and record your results. Write another rule that will allow you to sort the objects into three different piles. Sort them and record your results.

Try to make other rules for a different number of piles and perhaps excluding one item or more.

THE LIVING AND LEARNING ENVIRONMENT FOR THE OPEN CLASSROOM

"Finding Out About Clouds"

Cutting up old magazines, the teacher collected a number of pictures of clouds. Each picture was attached to a cardboard backing and labeled. All the pictures were filed in a box. A brief statement about clouds was pasted on the box:

There are all kinds of clouds. Some types have special names: cirrus, cumulus, nimbus, and stratus. Sometimes we use words together to describe clouds, e.g., alto-stratus, cumulo-nimbus. The pictures in the box show what each type of cloud looks like. Various kinds of clouds relate to different kinds of weather. Rain clouds look different from clouds on sunny days. Weathermen study clouds a great deal in their work. People whose work relates to a study of the weather are called meteorologists.

Separate cards suggested ideas for studies. Included were cards such as the following:

Make a record book of the kinds of clouds you observe over the next several days. Your record might include data similar to the following:

Date

—Type of cloud
—Drawing of some of its shapes
—How much of the sky was covered? (spotty, about ¼, about ½, nearly all)
—Temperature
    at 9:00 A.M.   at 1:00 P.M.
—Wind Direction

Devise an experiment to see if you can make clouds. (Hint: Look in the science experiment book for ideas on how to do this.)

Cut several pictures with clouds from a magazine and use these to write a story. You might start the story by looking at one picture and then look at another picture to develop another part of the story, a third picture for another part, and so on. Try to include in your story reference to the clouds and how they affect the moods and feelings people have.

> Try to find pictures of clouds other than those in the sky, for example, pictures that show clouds of smoke, of insects, and so on. Put together a "Cloud Book."

"Weighing Center"

Included would be several types of weighing instruments—bathroom scale, spring scale, balance, fish weights of various weights (they come in all gradations from fractions of an ounce to a pound or more), and postal scale. Various materials to be weighed could be on hand in various boxes. Include also such objects as bricks (concrete and clay) and containers to scoop up various amounts of sand, rice, beans, dirt, and so on.

Various types of work cards might be developed. Ideas such as the following could be developed into cards:

You and Your Weight

1. How much do you weigh? Who is lighter, who is heavier than you? Record all results.
2. Test how hard you can press on the bathroom scale with a finger. Your hand. Your right foot (keeping the other foot on the floor). Make a record showing how you and your friends compare. You might want to show each person's results like this:

Total Weight of Person	Pressure by One Finger	Pressure by One Hand	Other

Look at your chart carefully. Write some statements about the relationship of the total weight of the person and the pressure results.
3. Weigh each shoe. Compare the weights of your shoes to those of other children's shoes. Make statements about the weight of shoes and the size, the kind of shoe, or some other factor.

Making a Scale

1. See if you can make a scale to weigh things by using the balance and fish weights. Test out the weight of special objects using your new scale, a bathroom scale, and the postal scale. Record your results. What else might you do?
2. Get two or three rubber bands, a box of fish weights, several small objects to weigh, and a large sheet of paper. Hang up the piece of paper with a nail. Now hang the rubber band from the nail and, using fish weights, make a mark to show how far the band stretches

for ½ ounce, 1 ounce, 1½ ounces, on up to 8 ounces. Using these markings hang several objects from the rubber band to see how much they weigh. Record your results. Test your findings by weighing the same objects on another scale.

3. Try using different sizes of rubber bands to make a scale. What do you observe about the size of the rubber bands and the effect of their size on the scale's markings (amount of stretch)? See if you can find out the strength of various rubber bands.

All About Weighing

1. Find out the weight of several objects. Record your results. Test your answers by weighing the same object on another type of scale.
2. Using one of the available containers find out how much it weighs when full of sand, rice, dirt, or other things. Write down what you find out.
3. Make a list of things that balance. Your list might look like this:
   —One shoe balances two cups of rice.
   —The 3-ounce fish weight balances 30 marbles.

Investigative learning centers and general theme-work areas make the classroom an exciting place for discovery, experimentation, and investigation. The environment is focused on primary materials for children to manipulate, observe, and use in various ways. Many books are available and serve as rich supports for children to use for reference. But books take a secondary position in the discovery-learning classroom. They are utilized as sources of information, fulfilling the function for which they are best designed. Children refer to books when they can contribute to the learning developing from experiences with primary materials. Books in this context contribute immeasurably to the quality of learning. Without them, much of the richness of the material-oriented environment would be impaired.

PROBLEMS, QUESTIONS, AND CONCERNS

As teachers think about and make tentative moves toward refocusing the classroom environment, many questions and concerns must be considered. Anticipation of these helps the teacher to handle problems when they arise. Discouragement and feelings of "why try" may be lessened during the initial period. And in some cases failures or seeming failures can be avoided.

INFORMAL TEACHING IN THE OPEN CLASSROOM

How many centers to start with is a frequently raised question. Obviously, many variables can be considered—the number of children, the size of the classroom, the energy of the teacher, the quantity of materials available, the time to be allowed for use, the type of initial schedule during changeover, and on and on. However, there is one factor that seems to stand out as most important: one center would tend to create problems of scheduling. Provide one "goody" and children scramble for it, creating a mess of subsidiary problems. Also, one center doesn't help children get used to making choices and taking responsibility for decisions. Probably two or three centers would have the same drawbacks in the usual size classroom with the usual number of children and it is probably better to start with four or five or more.

The teacher can begin in two phases: first, reorganizing the classroom to reflect general theme-work areas and then adding the investigative learning centers. To develop these the teacher might begin with a large box for each planned center and over a period of time toss materials and possible starter ideas (rough questions) into the box. As the box begins to fill the teacher might take time to organize and prepare it for the classroom. After enough centers have been developed, all can be taken to the classroom and set up in final form. When this is done the teacher can launch into introducing a new way of working to the class.

How and where to get a variety of materials and equipment are other problems. With limited school budgets teachers often have few or no funds to purchase learning items. Frequently the teacher is faced with having to scrounge or even to spend personal funds. Fortunately, however, although time and effort are involved, it is possible to locate all kinds of free material for classrooms. Parents are a primary source. A letter to each parent outlining needs often produces a wealth of junk, furniture, and so on. One school head[1] described an unusual source—the trash collector. Monthly he swung by the school and dumped a load of trash for the children to sort through for "finds."

---

[1]Audrey Sutton, *Ordered Freedom* (Encino, Calif.: The International Center for Educational Development, 16161 Ventura Blvd., 1970).

THE LIVING AND LEARNING ENVIRONMENT FOR THE OPEN CLASSROOM

Some teachers in search of materials have reported excellent results with the following sources:

- Apartment and large office buildings—frequently the landlord recarpets for each new tenant. In a business building recarpeting may be done because of the decorating ideas of the new lessee. Therefore, the old discarded carpet is sometimes quite good.

- Garage sales—ads in newspapers are filled with "garage sales." Many times the leftovers will be given free to a teacher. Even the price to buy is usually quite reasonable.

- Salvage and junk yards are filled with useful learning materials.

- Large business offices are frequently good sources of discarded business machines. Most firms have a depreciation policy related to such equipment and after a stated number of years machines are automatically replaced. Old ones are junked (sometimes in working order).

- Car and other transportation dealers are frequently good sources of intriguing packing material. For example, motorcycles are shipped completely encased in molded styrofoam. These large pieces make excellent bases for art projects, inventions, storage, and so on.

- Building contractors and demolition companies are good sources of discarded items, victims of new construction or "making way for progress."

The hunt for materials need not be the teacher's job alone. The children can be involved too. With imagination and searching fascinating items can be brought into the classroom. The yellow pages of the phone book are worthwhile to look through as one thinks about "what I can get where."

Noise does change as children are freed to engage in purposeful activity. How much noise there will be and its effect on classroom functioning should be considered. Frequently the real problem is the teacher. The expectation of the past was of a quiet classroom. The teacher, therefore, may worry that noise will be misunderstood or that it will handicap learning. The teacher, too, is probably far more sensitive to noise than the children are. This does not mean, of course, that the "crash, bang," harsh type of noise is acceptable. Rather, there seems to be a "hum" in a classroom where children are actively engaged in projects and studies that have meaning for them.

The noise problem, however, seems to disappear with time. At first it is disturbing, but as new routines are established and the teacher sees learning developing, concerns diminish. At the start it may be helpful to plan for a quiet period or two during the day. Another solution could be a bell that the children are free to ring when the noise level becomes disturbing. (At first the bell ringing may be more of a problem than the noise, so frequent class discussion may be needed.) If noise is indeed a problem, then possible solutions should stem from class discussion and analysis of the situation. The teacher should not become the sole judge and enforcer. Rather the group involved ought to suggest, test, and arrive at reasonable guides.

Discipline problems in the materials-centered classroom do occur. At first there is greater likelihood of misuse of materials, especially if in the past books have been the only prominent materials. Now that the children are free to do things such as squirt water, launch gliders, or roll around on the floor, mishaps and mischievous behavior can occur. Sometimes it's necessary to remove a material and perhaps reintroduce it after the children have become more adept at working in a stimulating environment. Reasonable rules can be developed. But it is better to involve the children in the development. For example, the problem is presented and discussed. Solutions are offered. Finally one or two are selected for testing. (If they work, fine; if not, the process continues.) Rules should be flexible and reasonable. The standard rules listed so frequently in conventional classrooms are neither effective nor developed on the basis of children's real thinking. The abandonment of a rule should occur when it becomes ineffective. A listing of ineffective rules serves only to show how unreal a classroom can be.

Use of equipment can be regulated by sensible procedures that can change and that relate to the individual. Before a child knows how to use a piece of equipment it is sensible for him to check first with the teacher when he wants to use it. Specific instructions and practice sessions can be developed to help children learn how to use equipment properly. After a child has demonstrated competence, checking with the teacher before use can be eliminated.

If materials are introduced at the point of need, mishandling may be reduced. For example, some materials, such as matches, may be better controlled by the teacher; i.e., made available only when needed for a particular study. Other materials may be modified by the teacher to prevent damage or harm. The electric cord of an appliance, no longer functioning properly, can be removed to prevent possible shocks or burns as children try to fix or disassemble it. Problems that do develop should be the grist of children's thinking and work in solving.

Cleaning up and "janitor's dismay" are problems that need careful thought by the teacher. The materials-discovery-oriented classroom is no housekeeper's joy. With loads of equipment, centers, large-scale pupil projects, increased scraps and waste, and an area broken up into smaller work areas, the classroom cleanup is not an easy task. Certainly the teacher should consider the custodian's problem, talk to him, and elicit recommendations. Will chairs on the tables help? Would cleaning "once over lightly" everyday be better than cleaning once a week? What could the class do to help? Frequent discussions with the custodian can help to ease the cleaning problems and often prevent other problems that can occur if the custodian feels that "messiness is not next to learning."

Cleanup, straighten-up, put-up time must be part of the daily routine. Frequently better results are obtained if this involves everyone and is not specifically related to one's own mess. Some teachers find that a detailed list of jobs (one for each child) on a large chart with a rotation system of assignments works best. At least it prevents the other problem, "Who left the books on the floor?" or "I didn't spill it so why should I clean it up? I cleaned up my things."

The class should be expected to return all materials to their proper storage area, pick up all scraps from tables and floors, arrange books and papers neatly, and take care of special cleaning, such as wiping up spills or even vacuuming carpets. Although active learning does indeed result in mess and materials strewn out during the process, the open classroom at the end of the day can be picked up and returned to order for the next day's work.

CONCLUSION

A classroom environment designed for good living and learning is a beehive of activity. Subjects, timetables, and assignments are replaced by projects, studies, and activities that interest the children and expand their learning. Time wasting, the glazed look, and disruptive behavior give way to involvement and finding out. Learning is exciting, for it involves observing and watching things happen, handling and working with materials and living things, taking apart and examining things, meeting and solving problems, creating and constructing, and expressing ideas and findings. But all of this does not happen by itself. The teacher is an important resource, facilitator, guide, and positive interventionist. The setting is good for living and learning but the teacher makes an important difference in the full impact of the use.

CHAPTER 3

Patterns for Pupil Decision Making and Planning

There is an entirely different quality in the classroom climate when organization and management procedures focus on creating a structure for freedom. Replacing external teacher ordering and conditioning with pupil self-ordering and growth in personal decision making alters essential elements in building a climate for living and working together. Differing work rhythms, differing time spans of involvement, and differing work directions quickly emerge as children become their own agents for learning. The task is to develop basic patterns of planning and living that promote individual development and yet prevent chaos. There is structure so that children are free

- To think.

- To talk and discuss ideas and activities.

- To experiment with materials and new ways of working.

- To move in individual ways to do work they have chosen and are excited about.

- To form groups based on common purpose and interests for working and sharing.

INFORMAL TEACHING IN THE OPEN CLASSROOM

- To have ready access to the human and material resources of the class, the school, and the community.

Opportunities for pupil involvement in classroom decisions and the development of responsibility for self-direction are basic starters. Neither will occur automatically; both can be difficult in initial attempts to move toward a plan of open education focusing on personal teaching and learning.

PUPIL DECISION MAKING

Classrooms are logical places for children to experiment with decision making, to evaluate decisions made, and to test insights and understandings in practical and meaningful ways. How often teachers rob children of opportunities for growth by taking over the record keeping, assigning, outlining steps to follow, establishing rules, and grading outcomes.[1] It's as though children are expected to learn how to swim without going into the water. The level of functioning in the dimensions of self-direction and responsibility are evident through pupils' daily questions: "What am I supposed to do?" "I've finished reading, now what?" "How long does the report have to be?" "I'm all done, can I go now?" "How many problems must I do?"

It's apparent that following directions and fulfilling teacher prescriptions add little to the child's growth in responsible decision making. He needs to be actively involved in creating his own system of learning if he is to become his own best teacher. An involvement must include things that really count. One doesn't really learn much about decision making by making insignificant choices and decisions. Weighing the alternatives, predicting possible consequences, making inferences, and evaluating outcomes in multiple dimensions on important problems and concerns are what provide ideas and insights.

The teacher may be convinced of the importance of pupil involvement in learning decisions and acceptance of individual

---

[1]See Bernice J. Wolfon, *Moving Toward Personalized Learning and Teaching* (Encino, Calif.: International Center for Educational Development, 1969), pp. 45-55.

responsibility, yet the question of how to move in these directions remains. Some children will at first be concerned about planning and choosing their own work. There may be frequent questions and continued seeking for approval by children who are unsure. Other children given the opportunity for more involvement will avoid tasks that demand sustained effort. They will choose simple tasks, limit their involvement to short-term activities, or create minor disturbances. We can't expect that children will automatically want to make decisions or that the decisions made will be those with which we would necessarily agree. Aimless activity and even boredom may easily result if careful thought is not given to an overall pattern for growth.

Recognizing these problems and realizing that at first children may be skeptical of increased opportunities to make choices, the teacher moving into open classroom teaching thinks through a new way of working as it might be developed with each individual child.

To begin with, it helps to consider two broad questions: "What learning decisions can be made?" and "Who will make the decisions?"

Important learning decisions are made in four major phases of a task: goal setting, plans for action, implementation or action, and evaluation. Each can be clarified with a series of questions:

1. Goal setting: What shall I learn? What shall I study? What shall I do? The "what" is at the heart of learning.
2. The learning plan: Which book shall I use? Which materials shall I use? Where shall I start? Shall I allot a few minutes or lots of time? Shall I do it until I finish or on a scheduled basis? What plans must I make to accomplish my goal? Answers to these and similar questions shape the kind of plan to be used in proceeding with the chosen task.
3. Action: At the beginning, the plan for learning may be somewhat sketchy. It tends to evolve as we get into the action part, doing things. Another whole series of questions may then emerge: Shall changes be made in the plan? Are new resources needed? What other kinds of things might be done? The action aspect may alter previous decisions about the *what* (goals) as well as the *how* (plan).

INFORMAL TEACHING IN THE OPEN CLASSROOM

4. Evaluation: How well did the plan work? How satisfying is the accomplishment? What changes should be made? Evaluation not only looks backward through the goals, the plan, and the action but also moves forward. From evaluation, new goals, new plans, and new actions evolve. Did it work well? Were you happy with it? Would you choose it again? Answers to these kinds of questions form the data useful in future choice-making.

FIGURE 3-1

Levels of Decision Making "Who makes the decision?"	Decision-Making Phases "What decisions can be made?"			
	Goal "What"	Plan "How"	Action "Doing"	Evaluation "Results"
Level 4 **Pupil**—develops options, teacher is resource. **Pupil**—decides, using teacher as needed.				
Level 3 **Teacher and Pupil**—develop alternatives. **Pupil**—decides in concert with teacher.				
Level 2 **Teacher**—states choices. **Pupil**—selects.				
Level 1 **Teacher**—suggests and decides. **Pupil**—"cops out."				

Decisions in each of these phases could be defined and elaborated on more fully. To think through these opens up possibilities for greater pupil involvement in decision making.

"Who decides?" is the next step to be considered. Four levels can help to clarify the role of teachers and pupils and directions for opening up the system.

INFORMAL TEACHING IN THE OPEN CLASSROOM

1. *Teacher Decides—Pupil "Cops Out."* Much classroom decision-making freedom operates at this low level. The
   teacher says, "Now, children, wouldn't you like to do some
   reading now?" "Yes," they chorus. "Let's open our books to
   page 26," the teacher directs. Then, "Read quietly until I
   call your group." Later, of course, we can depend on the
   adult to decide whether the experience has been bad, good,
   or indifferent. The pupil has not been basically involved
   except to "follow directions." He has been a receiver,
   listening while the teacher has worked very hard to establish
   the goal, make the plan, enforce the action, and record the
   results. The child hasn't had to be involved at all; he has had
   a glorious, nonthinking day!

2. *Teacher Gives Choices—Pupil Selects.* Presenting choices is a
   second level of decision making. The teacher asks, "Would
   you like to read or do math now?" The child may
   legitimately select his preference or choose between alternatives. Though the big decisions are made by the teacher, the
   child has for a moment had some degree of involvement.
   Frequently it is debatable whether the choices are significant. "Would you like to read your reader or your
   storybook?" If the child doesn't want to read, he's in hot
   water, because he *has* to read. All he can really choose is the
   book—and the choice between books may not be much of an
   alternative. This level can easily become meaningless if
   choices are not perceived as important by the pupil. At best,
   the pupil selects. He has not had to think of an alternative or
   suggest possibilities for a learning experience.

3. *Teacher and Pupil Suggest Possibilities.* This is a fairly big
   leap in decision making. The teacher and the child discuss
   alternatives and possibilities. Ideas come from both. The
   teacher moves to keep the decision open until two or three
   good ideas are "on the table." The attempt is to get the child
   to see that although he started with but one choice (or one
   alternative), there are really many kinds of possibilities.

   After ideas are suggested, the next step is to make a
   final choice. The child is free to choose an idea he suggested
   or one suggested by the teacher. The choice may or may not
   be the best as viewed by the teacher, but at least the child
   was aware of possibilities other than his beginning idea.

4. *Pupil Suggests Possibilities.* At this level the child can really

suggest such a range of options that there is no need of throwing in other possibilities. If a child has thought of two or three very good possibilities, there's no point in thinking of another half dozen. When a child chooses one of the possibilities, he has made a decision. He is constantly improving his own sense of awareness and processes of choice making. He uses the teacher as a resource for ideas or to help clarify an idea.

Viewing pupil decision making in light of these phases and levels of "who decides" the teacher can begin to think about how to increase the individual pupil's responsibility for learning actions. Different patterns of involvement for different children can be tried. For Margaret, a beginning might be to ask her to select from suggested alternatives (Level 2) of the planning phase. At other phases the teacher suggests and decides (Level 1).

Jim, Harvey, and Sue can be involved at Level 2 in all the learning phases. Marilyn and Michele can be involved at Level 3 in the planning and action phase and at Level 2 in the other phases. And so it goes, individual starting places for individual pupils.

The teacher's level of comfort must also be considered. At first the chief reason for not moving toward greater pupil involvement may be the uncertainty of the teacher. Perhaps the teacher decides that opportunity for pupil decision making will be restricted to the planning phase at the level of selecting a choice from teacher alternatives. After testing and gaining some assurance that "children can handle this," the teacher decides to allow choice in another phase or two. From here the switch may be to even greater flexibility based upon individual children's moving at different speeds.

The progress toward greater and greater pupil involvement in learning decisions continues in ways that are productive and comfortable for both teacher and pupils. There is, of course, no smooth gradual development. Rather, progress is uneven, scattered with occasional "clamp-downs" by the teacher or even requests from a pupil now and then for the teacher to direct or decide. But the intent and direction are clear—personal involvement in making learning decisions and growth in responsible self-direction. With experience and confidence, opportunities

INFORMAL TEACHING IN THE OPEN CLASSROOM

can be increased by moving in additional phases and operating at increasingly pupil-directed levels. Thus, choices and decisions can become an important part of the school experience.

TEACHER PLANNING—THE DAILY RESOURCE GUIDE

To help children grow in thinking and planning abilities, a master resource guide is valuable. It establishes a general class pattern to be used as a starting phase for the development of personal plans and commitments. Constructing the guide is a major teacher function and replaces the typical sterile teaching plan found frequently in conventional practice.

The resource guide embodies several key elements:

- It is flexible and is built daily.

- It is built on pupil needs observed by the teacher as he works with individual pupils.

- It takes advantage of current pupil interests, daily happenings, and pupil excitements.

- It focuses on problems and questions real to the children involved.

- It emphasizes "starting points" rather than "coverage."

Because the guide will have a major influence on the pattern of the day's work, sensitive and imaginative thought should be given to its development. Three major parts serve as a basic format:

- Constraints and requirements.

- Resources and opportunities.

- Starters—suggestions for investigations and studies.

Constraints and requirements include the fixed points and

"together times" for the day, such restrictions as those imposed because of facilities and resources, and the requirements that deal with limiting pupil choices.

General school schedules include fixed points that facilitate the working of the entire school. The individual teacher generally has little control over these but they do affect how the classroom functions. The lunch period may be fixed for each class so that the cafeteria can prepare and serve food within a reasonable amount of time. Recess may be required and fixed for the school in order to allow for playground supervision and provide teacher breaks. An assembly may be called at eleven o'clock. School may be on an early dismissal schedule for the day. These "fixed points," regular and special, are not directly controlled by the teacher but do influence the daily work flow of the class. In the resource guide the special fixed points are noted. Probably after a few days of school the regular points are omitted becuase everyone is familiar with them. Even so, they are to be reckoned with in terms of planning.

"Together times" are different. They are established by the teacher to build a feeling of community among the class and to consolidate work that is being developed by the class. The times may vary each day, but ordinarily the class comes together as a unit one or two times a day. Examples would include the planning session, the evaluation period, story time, a general class sharing time, a special time for discussion—a "town" meeting, for example. These times are noted on the guide so that children can expect these interruptions in the day's flow and can plan their work accordingly.

Constraints are also imposed because of limited facilities or resources. "There is one movie projector; our time for using it is between 10:00 and 11:00." "The music teacher will work with the chorus between 1:00 and 1:30 today." "Books may be checked out from the bookmobile at 1:00 today." In some cases the constraining factor may be that if the pupil wants to participate, he'll have to start at an appointed time, not when he chooses. Other constraints may be more in the nature of everyone's having to participate.

Another type of constraint is that which deals with "closing down" on pupil choices. Frequently, in the initial stages teachers feel uncomfortable removing all requirements.

INFORMAL TEACHING IN THE OPEN CLASSROOM

There are fears that children would not do math if it's not required. Or the question "Don't we have to make sure each child reads so much each day?" is frequently asked. Most fears are related to skills, and there's little doubt that efforts along these lines are exaggerated in terms of actual need or usefulness to the individual child. Skill learning is better taught to the individual. Small groups may be organized to include those children who need help in a certain area in order to move forward in a lively study or topic they are investigating.

As teachers begin to see that a child does involve himself with reading, with math, with writing in useful ways, requirements should diminish. Any closure on choice and decision making should largely be confined to an individual child, perhaps through the individual conference, rather than generalizing a teacher-felt need to a whole class.

Resources and opportunities are listed to show today's possibilities clearly. Special events, demonstrations, and exhibits are noted. For activities such as knitting instruction, guitar lessons, or oil painting techniques, volunteer parents and community citizens acting as special resources are listed. And here is the place the teacher announces how he will work with small groups today, what direct instructional sessions are planned, or what demonstrations are featured. He says in effect, "Here are the special direct ways I plan to contribute to the resources available for today." Children are clued in to the possibilities for working with the teacher.

Some opportunities are in the form of skill sessions, others might be discussion sessions, still others might open up new interests when the teacher starts a science experiment or relates an experience such as a recent trip. And, of course, the individual one-to-one conference times are listed. In some cases, teachers will initiate these conferences, but the whole class knows that if anyone wants to confer with the teacher, here are the possible times that it can be arranged.

Starters—Suggestions for possible studies and investigations are an important facet for the development of an open education program. Here we begin to help children enlarge their perceptions about possibilities and opportunities for learning. The focus is experience rather than filling time with fractionalized "subjects." The experience will be deeper for some pupils than others, but for all it will be built on personal interests so that minds are stretched, imaginations alerted, and senses exercised. Each child develops a personal response in the acquisition of knowledge and skills.

FIGURE 3-2

Today's Guide		
Constraints and Requirements	Resources and Opportunities	Starters
Schedule 30 minutes for reading skill development. Allot time to work on individual science project. P.E. 11:00–11:30. Class Town Meeting, 11:30. Write a story. Bring individual records up to date.	Special event in resource room (see announcement). Skill session on locating and using references, 10:00. Skill session on multiplication patterns, 10:20. Film on planetary system shown at 1:00 in auditorium (30 min.). How to use the video recorder, 2:00. Individual conferences 9:00 – 10:00 and 1:00–2:00.	Cloud shaped like a horse—making a study of cloud patterns; making clouds, songs and poems about clouds; effect of clouds on people's feelings; kinds of clouds; how fast clouds travel. . . . How big a "wind" are you? (Note science area.) Equipment tearing up street—making a mural of man and his machines; doing a historical study on streets; facts and figures about streets in our town; doing a study to test skidding on various surfaces.

Initially, many ideas for interesting studies will come from the teacher. Some may develop from the happenings, experiences, or objects brought or contributed by the children. Starting points are endless—an insect, equipment tearing up the street, a windy day, a new baby, a trip, a shiny rock, a colored leaf, a cloud formation, a new toy, a loud noise, a peculiar smell, a fish, a visit from grandparents, and on and on. Questions, such as "What did you see on the way to school?" "What interesting thing happened to you since yesterday?" "Where did you go last night?" encourage children to bring ideas into the classroom. Here we're not talking about sharing as an activity but rather to get ideas on what has relevance and what is of current interest so that we can talk about possible studies. We take whatever it is. With the class we explore possibilities to get ideas for possible starting points for the day.

The webbing of ideas illustrates the potential that any

observation, interest, or object may have for study. Questions and ideas range freely over a wide field. Subject barriers are broken down and yet integrated quite naturally. Suggested ideas may be explored by individuals or in small groups on a personal choice basis. Sometimes a group project such as an exhibit, mural, or dramatization results naturally as a way to bring all the studies together in some related way. The flow of interests and questions from an observation may develop in such a way as that illustrated in Figure 3-3.

The teacher builds the master resource guide from data collected during work with children. Individual pupil-teacher conferences, class discussions, conversations with children during their work, and observation of children at play all provide information of value to the sensitive, aware teacher. Shared excitement, questions, and requests for help furnish additional clues. The general flow of the day and points brought out in the evaluation period offer further guidance. Using this growing fund of knowledge, the teacher ponders resources and opportunities that can help children build on growing edges of learning, experiences that will clinch beginning discoveries, and ideas that will enlarge perceptions and interests. Some parts of the guide can be put together at the close of a day in preparation for the next day, but other parts must wait for the children—what they bring that's fresh, vital, and of interest to them.

The master resource guide emphasizes pupil planning and decision making. It promotes the idea of experiments, investigations, and wise use of resources to promote individual growth. Using relevant information from the resource guide, the pupil begins to think out what he intends to pursue and how. A commitment is made. The order, structure, or plan is one that promotes freedom so that a group can function in a classroom workshop where time schedules are pupil determined, where pupils make real choices about their learning and "get on with it."

DAILY PLANNING

Daily planning periods help everyone get started. This is a time for setting individual work plans. Attention is called to the master resource guide. Ideas for possible investigations and

FIGURE 3-3

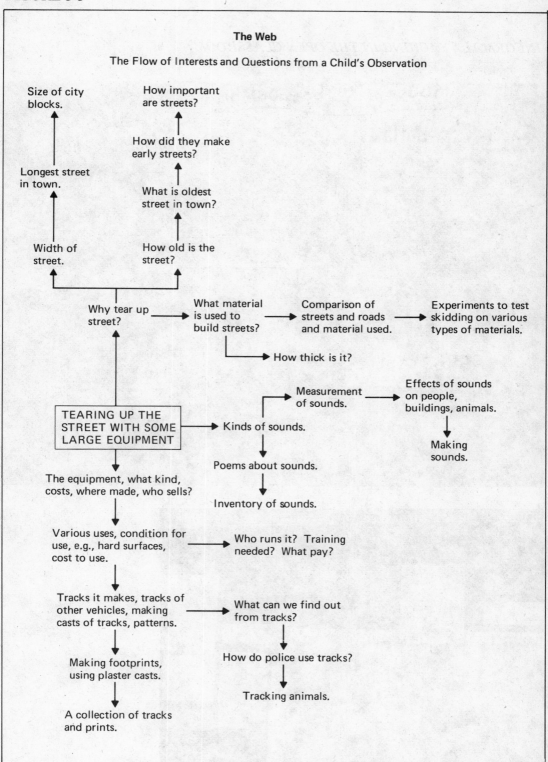

The Web

The Flow of Interests and Questions from a Child's Observation

Size of city blocks.

How important are streets?

How did they make early streets?

Longest street in town.

What is oldest street in town?

Width of street.

How old is the street?

Why tear up street?

What material is used to build streets?

Comparison of streets and roads and material used.

Experiments to test skidding on various types of materials.

How thick is it?

Measurement of sounds.

Effects of sounds on people, buildings, animals.

TEARING UP THE STREET WITH SOME LARGE EQUIPMENT

Kinds of sounds.

Making sounds.

Poems about sounds.

The equipment, what kind, costs, where made, who sells?

Inventory of sounds.

Various uses, condition for use, e.g., hard surfaces, cost to use.

Who runs it? Training needed? What pay?

Tracks it makes, tracks of other vehicles, making casts of tracks, patterns.

What can we find out from tracks?

Making footprints, using plaster casts.

How do police use tracks?

A collection of tracks and prints.

Tracking animals.

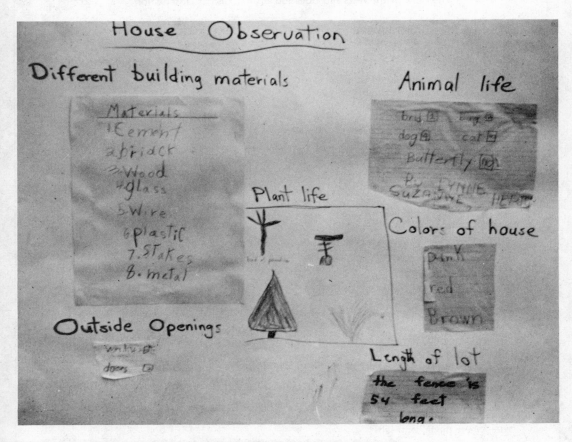

studies are added to the guide. Arrangements to get needed resources are made.

Children come into the classroom with experiences, interests, capabilities, and spontaneity. They, themselves, are additional resources to bring into planning and in carrying out plans. Children are encouraged to talk about how they will spend their time, what they are finding out. Individual children share their plans. Ralph talks about his study of butterflies. Chris asks if anyone wants to work with her on a mural she wants to make about "Homes Around The World." Sandy talks about a play she's writing. John is constructing an Indian village. Sheila and Melanie need help with an experiment they're doing with a pendulum. From listening to a few classmates talk about their plans and needs, other children get ideas. The teacher begins to get a picture of directions and developments. He adds an idea, suggests a possible resource, clarifies a hazy plan, and asks needed questions.

After a few minutes children who have "firmed up" their plans are encouraged to get started. With the smaller remaining groups the teacher can offer additional guidance, perhaps giving specific suggestions from which children will choose. In this way no one is held up, waiting until everyone is ready. And yet there is time spent as a group, contributing to the feeling of community.

Planning periods vary in length. At the early stages this period is apt to be longer, until the class becomes familiar with individual planning. Time is not so important if interest is high. If children can start as plans are "firmed up," there is flexibility and the teacher's attention can be focused where help is most needed. At first it may even be desirable to have two planning periods, one in the morning and one after a break or after lunch. This can be especially useful if the children are younger. The second period might be optional so the individual child can decide whether or not he wants to participate.

As the day begins with planning a good way to close the day is with an evaluation period. Such a session gives the children an opportunity to talk about what went well, how they worked, and what interesting things happened. Ideas for things to do might be listed for the next day's planning period. Children can call attention to special materials they'll need and solicit volunteer help. Learnings can be discussed and clarified so that children have ready answers when parents ask, "What did you learn in school today?"

The evaluation session is a time to weave together the loose ends of the day and to sharpen the focus for the next steps. It builds on recent experience to help children clarify productive ways of working as a group as well as individually. It takes note of the joys, savoring high points, and links together the various learnings so there is a "flow" of experiences.

USING PLANNING FORMS

Writing down plans and evaluative comments is especially useful while children are learning to take responsibility for managing their time and deciding what to do. Planning forms are helpful. There are numerous possibilities. In the initial stages of moving toward pupil planning, a form might include familiar subject areas and former working patterns. The student has some choice such as when to study a subject area and even what he will do in that subject. The important thing is that pupils begin to take on responsibility for thinking through their plan of action for learning.

Different forms can be used, even within a class. There is no need to have all students using the same kind. One type may be more suitable than another for a particular pupil. Some children can immediately move into the more open type of planning guides (Samples 1, 2, 3, and 4). Others will need more specific guidelines, such as time blocks (Sample 5) or subject blocks (Samples 6 and 7), for initial experiences. Whatever the type used, the idea is to begin to involve the child in the pattern of the day's work and to record sufficient data for a later assessment of planning effectiveness. For many children a written plan serves to strengthen the commitment to follow through.

Even very young children can begin the process of recording plans. They can respond to pictures representing areas of work and check their choices for the day (Samples 8 and 9). Older children can use more complicated forms, but the planning must not become a burdensome chore. Essentially, the planning guide is a brief record of the overall scheme. Checks by activities, simple phrases or words to indicate intentions, and general direction are all that is needed.

The planning forms, if kept from day to day and week to week, build a picture of a child's work at school. As such, the form becomes a valuable tool to review at conference time, to share with parents, and to use periodically as raw data for charting and graphing "how I spent my time in school."

To keep these guides, a simple manila folder can be used. The current plan sheet is stapled on top of old ones on one side. A sheet for "comments" can be fastened on the other side.

During the day the child probably keeps his plan folder with him and stores it at the end of the school day in a box or file drawer in the classroom. In this way the teacher can review a few plan folders each day and use data from them as a basis for a conference the next day or as a basis for general comments during the next day's planning period.

During the day the teacher will frequently look at individual plan sheets while working with the children. It isn't necessary to check the plan sheet each day for each child. Problems soon become evident and as they do an individual conference on planning is far more meaningful than the checking process. Questions are to be answered, helpful hints tossed out (Sample 10), and in every way the teacher stands ready to help. But checking verges more on the negative than the positive. The teacher's actions should let the children know, "I trust you. I'm here to act as a resource and to help when you need me."

Obviously, initial plans as well as specific plans later on will not be perfect. There will be pitfalls. These, though, become the basis for analyzing what went wrong and why. New ideas emerge that can be tried to see if they work. It's important that children gain power in planning and this comes about by doing it, looking at what has been done in some rational way, and then trying new patterns.

There are many factors to consider in developing a good plan—"How I feel today," "What experience I'm building on," "What job I'm tackling" are a few. The number of questions asked and the data gathered influence the final result. Young children naturally ask fewer questions and consider less data than older children. Time pressures can influence the amount of data to be gathered. And of course the importance attached to what is being planned has an effect. All of this is part of planning.

Through planning the classroom takes on structure. But the structure is personal and individual, yet developed to mesh with the group. For the child planning helps to stress the need to

- Give thought to what he's going to do.

- Make a commitment to *his choice*.

- Develop ideas about time, materials, and resources for carrying out what he has planned.

SAMPLE 1

DAILY PLAN

NAME: _____   DATE: _____

Schedule for Day (General Plan)

_____

_____

_____

_____

_____

_____

_____

_____

_____

_____

Evaluation (What didn't you finish? What did you enjoy most? What are the possible ideas for to-morrow? and so on.)

_____

_____

_____

_____

_____

_____

_____

_____

_____

_____

_____

_____

SAMPLE 2

DAILY PLAN

DATE: _____   NAME: _____

PLANS FOR TODAY	EVALUATION (GENERAL COMMENTS)

DATE
PLANS FOR TODAY	EVALUATION (GENERAL COMMENTS)

SAMPLE 3

PLAN SHEET FOR (SUBJECT) _____

NAME: _____ WEEK OF: _____

PLAN FOR THE DAY	RESULTS OF THE DAY	RESOURCES USED
MONDAY		
TUESDAY		
WEDNESDAY		
THURSDAY		
FRIDAY		

SAMPLE 4

MY WEEK'S WORK

NAME: _____ WEEK OF: _____

MONDAY _____
_____
_____
_____

TUESDAY _____
_____
_____
_____

WEDNESDAY _____
_____
_____
_____

THURSDAY _____
_____
_____
_____

FRIDAY _____
_____
_____
_____

Reading   boy Reading   Science   c-a-t- Spelling   Drama
           ball Skills

Listening   Art   2 Math   Story   Bueno! Spanish
                    +2

Tape Recorder   a a Handwriting   Puppets   Reading Games

SAMPLE 5

PLANNING GUIDE

NAME: _____ WEEK OF: _____

	MONDAY	TUESDAY	WEDNESDAY	THURSDAY	FRIDAY
9:00-9:15	OPENING BUSINESS ANNOUNCEMENTS PLANNING				
9:15-10:15					
10:15-10:30	RECESS				
10:30-11:30					
11:30-12:00	PHYSICAL EDUCATION				
12:00-12:45	LUNCH				
12:45-1:45					
1:45-2:00	RECESS				
2:00-2:30					STORY HOUR
2:30-2:45	EVALUATION				

SAMPLE 6A

DAILY PLAN

DATE: _____ NAME: _____

MONDAY	TUESDAY	WEDNESDAY	THURSDAY	FRIDAY
READING				
MATH				
LANGUAGE ARTS				
SCIENCE				
SOCIAL STUDIES				
OTHERS				

Name _____

Date _____

Periods	Read	Comments

Read

See me Go run

Comments
_____
_____
_____
_____
_____

Write

Aa

_____
_____
_____
_____
_____

Math

$2 + 2 = \boxed{4}$
$3 - 1 = \boxed{2}$

_____
_____
_____
_____
_____

Choice ?

_____
_____
_____
_____
_____

INFORMAL TEACHING IN THE OPEN CLASSROOM

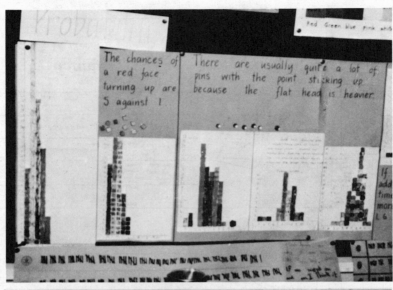

SAMPLE 7

SCHEDULE   Name: _____

Color what you do.

(Partner Reading)

(Ditto)   (Game)   (Job Card)

(Spelling)

(Test)

_____

(Math)

(Ditto)   (Job Card)   (Game)   (Measuring)

_____

(Story)   (Poem)   (Diary)

_____

(Project)   (Science)   (Map)   (Art)   (Music)

_____

Name _____

Day _____

Sea Life	Records
Library	Games
Write	Easel
Math	Type
Listen	Plays
Art	Music

SAMPLE 9

MY PLAN FOR LEARNING

1. <u>X</u> What I plan to do.
2. Ⓧ What I did.

	A.M.	P.M.
Listening Area		
Writing		
Games Center		
Reading		
Math		
Social Studies		
Science		
Art		
Special Interest		
Project Work		

P.M.	YES	NO
I learned new things today.		
I worked without disturbing others.		
I put things away.		

NAME _____

DATE _____

SAMPLE 10

DAILY PLANNING GUIDE

Helpful Hints

Plan to spend time in several areas each day. For example you might spend time in reading, mathematics, science, or writing. This helps you get in the habit of doing some work each day in a variety of subjects. You will want to look at what you did yesterday to get ideas of things you need to finish as well as to note areas you did not have time for so these can be scheduled in your plan for today.

Sometimes there are interruptions or activities scheduled that interfere with what you intended to do. When this happens, don't let it worry you. Plans can always be carried over to the next day. Schedule yourself one day at a time until you feel comfortable about making plans for longer periods.

You probably should not schedule all of your time. You may need some time to catch up with little bits and pieces here and there that you have not been able to complete. Sometimes a study takes a bit longer than anticipated and some free time on your schedule can take care of this. You may also want to have some free time for reading or just general exploring of new ideas.

Date	Time	Study Areas for Focus	Planning Notes Investigations, Activities, Experiments

ORGANIZATIONAL AND PLANNING PATTERNS IN LATER STAGES OF DEVELOPMENT

Extending the opportunity for choice and decision making to children may be first steps. But growth along this dimension is uneven, sporadic, and not necessarily desired by all. Children not used to making decisions cannot be expected to move quickly. Throwing off familiar patterns of following teacher directions and doing assignments may be difficult. Some children will "suspect" and go through a period of testing to see what the limits are. Others may confine their choices to what has been expected in the past. A few can be expected to be rash in their proposals. Still others will begin to respond openly and make attempts to tackle the challenge in productive ways.

Knowing this the teacher is prepared to act more rationally and seek to respond in individual ways to children. A big hurdle is to move away from approving or disapproving personal learning plans. With clear ground rules established such as (1) no destruction of property, (2) no physical harm to self or others, and (3) no infringement on the rights of others, the teacher is in a strong position to offer guidance in the development of plans and to monitor the progress made in carrying out a stated plan.

Marc writes on his plan, "Do nothing." Maybe he's testing the teacher. Maybe he wants time "to think," to consolidate learning or figure out the next step. Maybe his energy level is low. Whatever the reason, there is no abridging of basic

guidelines, so the teacher makes no response. A short time later, though, Marc is wandering around the room, quietly and without bothering others. Now the teacher moves, calmly, "Marc, what was your plan of action for this time?" The monitoring process takes over. Marc's attention is drawn to his plan. If it was "to do nothing" then wandering around does not fit. His option is either to return to the original decision or to change his plan. If Marc was testing the teacher then the teacher's behavior suggests not that a pupil can't "do nothing" or "wander" but that accountability to personal planning is expected.

Shelly decides to do no math today, the next day, or the third day. The teacher is faced with a question—how long can it be permitted? The actions of the teacher can say, "You guessed wrong, the opportunity to make choices and decisions does not include not doing what I think is necessary," or the decision can say, "I'm concerned, I want to see what factors you're weighing in making the decision but the final outcome is still up to you."

As the transfer of power from teacher direction to pupil direction becomes clearer and better understood, the quality of their decisions becomes a matter of concern to the pupils.

Helping children move from traditional types of work choices toward in-depth investigations and studies that have personal meaning must be tackled. Several questions can be raised at this point. Answers may give clues for the next steps.

- Does the planning form maintain the reference to subjects, to time slots?

- Are teacher requirements or constraints still focused on doing work in subjects, spending more time in typical conventional school ways?

- Has the room environment changed from the transitional phase of interest or learning centers toward becoming more of a laboratory-workshop-resource area?

- During the planning period is the focus moving toward the development of children's interests, questions, and observations?

PATTERNS FOR PUPIL DECISION MAKING AND PLANNING

Planning and scheduling take on a different character as children get used to making choices and managing their own time. After the first hurdles, as children begin to understand and accept individual responsibility and are freer to pursue individual interests, details of planning and scheduling must change. Importance is still attached to the idea of thinking through "what I want to do," "how I will do it," and "what the results were." But the more mechanical aspects of planning forms, the material resource guide, and other devices instituted to help in the transitional stages are reviewed and changed to meet new conditions.

Mike is quite sure of a study he wants to undertake. He wants to explore the making and workings of an automobile. The teacher and Mike have discussed resources, first steps, and possible developments and have made arrangements for periodic "talk" sessions about the work. An anecdotal entry in Mike's learning journal is made. There is no need for the usual daily planning form. It doesn't fit in this situation. The teacher realizes that specific time scheduling is not possible nor even desirable. Instead he will remain alert to possible current resources and will talk with Mike now and then, sometimes informally, at other times with a focus in mind, to determine progress, to add useful terminology, to link experiences, and to extend the inquiry.

In Mike's current study, as well as in others he will undertake, specific learning needs will arise. These needs may be in the form of skills—not just so-called basic skills, but skills of thinking, social relationships, problem solving, and so on—through which he will obtain a wider understanding of his world. At this point Mike and the teacher, working together, can develop plans to satisfy these needs, plans that may even call a temporary halt to the study under way. Teaching in a very direct way may be called for, a practice (or even drill) exercise may be helpful, outside assistance may be required, or Mike may well be able to solve the problem himself by following a plan that he and the teacher have worked out.

Mike is actively involved. His school day starts when he arrives. There is no need to wait around, nor does he need a signal to start. He can follow his own individual work rhythm freely during the day. The teacher is available for consultant help and for assistance in obtaining resources. For Mike school has shifted from a focus on covering subjects and activities to a focus on individual learning.

In the fully functioning open classroom planning then becomes more fluid and attuned to individual children and their development. Sometimes the plan is a conference and sometimes recording may be a simple anecdotal record. At other times a detailed plan carefully recorded may be instituted because there is a recognized need. Planning becomes a useful tool for the child as he seeks out experiences for growth.

Teachers, too, must be sensitive as to when to change, to lift ceilings, and to suggest new patterns if children are to move away from textbook, subject-oriented choices. At initial phases of transition, it may be enough to focus on helping children get accustomed to making choices and plans within the context of familiar, past experiences and expectations in school. Consequently, even though ideas that are not typical subject work are suggested, children may make most choices within the usual subject framework in order to gain familiarity with a new pattern of working. This is only a beginning in the transfer of learning power from teacher to pupil. Indirectly as well as directly, however, teachers can prevent fuller accomplishment.

Teachers need to work long and hard, to think through carefully the nature and purposes of schooling, and to become convinced that informal teaching in the open classroom is the better way if their attitude is not to be a handicapping factor. Reservations show through actions and are easily picked up by the children. This factor, obviously, would influence the kind of plans the children would make because many pupils are anxious "to please the teacher."

Although attitudes and reservations are frequently harder for the teacher to detect, direct teacher actions are sometimes not recognized. Consequently the teacher should take careful stock of the situation. For a starter, the whole planning process between children and teacher should be scrutinized. The master resource guide may be continuing to require certain subject work or to emphasize resources that are subject oriented. If the teacher is still not comfortable with the thought of no requirements, certainly a change might be acceptable. The constraint and requirement column might begin to reflect ideas such as are shown in Sample 11.

SAMPLE 11

MASTER RESOURCE GUIDE

CONSTRAINTS AND REQUIREMENTS	RESOURCES AND OPPORTUNITIES

Choose a topic and do a study

Automobiles	Lizards
Airplanes	Bees
Boats	Plants
Bats	Blood
Snakes	Homes
Dolls	Customs
Toys	Castles

In your studies, include answers to these questions:

1. What might you read and what can you find out about your topic from books available?
2. What mathematics can you do related to your study? (A scale drawing, a description based on various measurements, a mathematical comparison between your topic and another on the list, an imaginary view of your topic if you increased everything by 7 and another number of your choice, and so on.)
3. What experiments can you devise and perform related to your topic?
4. What can you find out by talking with people about your topic?

INFORMAL TEACHING IN THE OPEN CLASSROOM

In the resources and opportunities section of the guide, a review should be made to see how the teacher is making himself available. Are most of the listings related to direct teaching of basic skills? Are there listings that are not subject oriented, such as those in Sample 12?

During the planning period the teacher should be aware of the nature of the questions he asks and the emphasis he may be making by calling attention to certain plans. Because old patterns are not easily changed, it may be useful to do reversals, e.g., work on your study today, adding new information without using books. Or the planning period may change to a sharing period in which children, notified on the previous day, share the latest developments on the investigation they are conducting.

The planning process evolves and changes in character as the teacher and the children begin to shift toward new roles and gain new understandings of what can be done in school. The master resource guide, which initially helped to shift planning from a teacher's plan for all to individual plans made through personal choices, becomes less needed in a formalized way. Some device, of course, will be needed to call attention to resources and opportunities. This could be a special bulletin board where notices are posted not only by the teacher but also by pupils. Starter ideas may become less detailed and may originate more from the pupils than from the teacher. A display corner where things as well as ideas can be exhibited may be a core. Children are encouraged to contribute ideas they want to explore but haven't had time to get to yet or things they feel might be of interest to someone in the class.

As the children feel more comfortable about accepting responsibility for learning and can demonstrate capability in working productively on their own, the planning period can gradually become a "together time." It can be a time to find out what's going on in the classroom and how individuals can merge projects to make a group study and to raise questions about work that's under way.

The teacher continues to play a key role in the work and flow of the classroom. The orchestration of resource elements so that opportunities are available to the class at the point of need is crucial. This means the teacher anticipates directions of studies so that resources are at hand or can be easily secured.

SAMPLE 12

MASTER RESOURCE GUIDE

CONSTRAINTS AND REQUIREMENTS	RESOURCES AND OPPORTUNITIES
	Teaching session—"how to find out" without reading.
	New library exhibit—studies made by children in the school.
	Teaching session—how to make rubbings.
	Make a geodesic dome—see announcement.
	New material today—will it add to your study? (See display table.)

Obviously there is no way of always having exactly what is needed or even anticipating correctly all turns of events. Yet talks with the children about what they're doing, what they're finding out, and what they're thinking of, as well as skillful observation, provide valuable clues.

Another key facet of the teacher's role in developing useful studies is making the children aware of daily happenings in the world outside. For many children these events have little meaning. For others the smallest event may initiate much thought and spark a series of questions. It is important, then, that the teacher attempt to hook up "school work" with what's going on in the outside environment. Learning related to daily living becomes more personal and builds more solidly toward an understanding of occurrences not directly experienced. The teacher who is aware of the learning potential of the smallest observations can help children move toward studies that extend and develop interests in and deepen understandings about the world we live in.

The pattern of classroom organization, management, and planning varies for each teacher and each class. There is no end phase. Rather, the work and flow of the day changes and constantly evolves. The structure promotes freedom for each child to engage in meaningful exploration and discovery as he grows in learning. The teacher contributes, other pupils contribute, the school adds and provides, and the child takes, uses, and in turn contributes to others. But there is a growing feeling of being "my own best teacher" and having the power to solve problems, to think through ideas, and to manage himself responsibly and productively. A classroom rhythm that makes each day a "happening" on such a personal road is the criterion for constructing patterns of organization and management.

CHAPTER 4

The Teacher at Work

The teacher is an active participant in the life and work of the open informal classroom. He has the responsibility of making a vital environment and providing wide opportunity for pupil growth. Organization and management procedures must be set within the context of pupil freedom to foster self-direction and individual responsibility for actions. A feeling of community must be built among the group members. And the teacher works to develop an individual relationship with each child built upon respect, trust, and concern.

The teacher's contribution and positive intervention in the learning process is built upon close observation and personal knowledge of a pupil's growth. Watching the child explore materials, meeting and solving problems, and working with others provides evidence of the child's interests and needs. Conversations and discussions with the child add further insight. From these the teacher constructs his response, drawing upon both scholarship—operating within an intellectual framework— and personal relationship. Essentially the teacher knows that to love is not enough. He must be an intellectually authentic person, basing observations and interpretations upon knowledge.

In the open classroom the teacher moves away from the conventional role of director of learning and transmitter of

INFORMAL TEACHING IN THE OPEN CLASSROOM

knowledge. There is no attempt to get children to act in unison. The flow of knowledge is not from the teacher to the pupil. Instead the teacher begins to experiment with ways to stimulate investigation, to explore ways of responding to pupils' inquiries, and to sharpen skills in guiding thinking to build deeper meanings.

THE TEACHER AS A RESPONDER

Responding appropriately to children's queries is an effective teaching process. The informal classroom encourages children to talk and to ask questions. Much of children's talk, especially for the young child, requires no audience nor interaction from another. It is almost a continuous monologue, bringing on-going experience to the consciousness of the child. Such talk helps the child to assimilate the processes of selection and abstraction. The talk deepens the child's personal grasp of the situation much the same way as does painting, drawing, modeling, or constructing. The sensitive teacher will encourage the use of such talk and will be aware of the dynamics involved so as not to interfere.

At other times talk by the child is directed so that a response is needed. This is not always in the form of a question. Sometimes the teacher is expected to take the role of a thing, a person, or a doll and to respond in conversational ways. Through this process there is necessity for responses, but the response is largely shaped by the child as he initiates the talk. Over a span of time the child narrows the unknown and attaches reality. Responses by the teacher help to reflect the child's growing insight and open up new paths for exploration. Certainly "answers" are not needed nor does the teacher short-circuit the process by attempting to speed up or direct the talk. The questions children ask require different considerations. So frequently we want to give too much or we misinterpret the query:

● John asks, "What is this?" as he holds up a pair of calipers. But he means, "What do you use them for? I'm intrigued with the object. Can you give me ideas as to what I could do with them?"

- Mary asks, "How do you like my poem?" Does she want you to evaluate it? Is she asking you to suggest some guidelines for her to use for improving it? Is she saying, "Here is something I want to share with you because I think it's good"?

- Susan says, "How do you divide 498 by 3?" Does she just want the answer because the process at the moment is secondary to the answer that is needed for a study she's making? Is she saying, "I need to learn to do some dividing"?

These examples point out only a few dimensions related to the teacher acting as a responder. Experimentation on the part of the teacher builds up additional facets. Basically the job is to keep the focus on the child's study rather than "jumping up to teach." What is the child's intent? What is the relationship between the question and the child's action and thinking at the moment? What is an honest reaction rather than a response built on teacher purpose or some subtle manipulation? These are the kinds of questions that, carefully thought through, help the teacher learn how to respond in ways that are useful to the child seeking to fulfill his own purpose.

TEACHER TALK

Teachers should be good at talking with children. But too often "teaching" gets in the way. Over the years I've asked teachers to tell me about a recent conversation they've had with a pupil in their classroom. Frequently, at first, they're stumped because they feel the whole day has been one of talking with children. But with persistence they begin to describe an episode. Nearly always the first response has to do with a child who is sharing something with the teacher. The teacher's part of the conversation usually includes something like "Thank you, Susie. I like that. You've done a nice job." Here I interrupt. "No, don't tell me about an incident in which you largely focused on being judgmental or evaluative. Just describe a discussion between you and a child as two equal individuals."

Another incident sometimes described is one in which the teacher's role is focused toward trying subtly to manipulate the child. Other conversations related emphasize the teacher's attempts to motivate a pupil, interest him in some idea or project, or cajole him into finishing up, hurrying up, or getting ready to start a new task. And so it goes. "Teaching" is so much in the way that very few teachers can recall a single lively conversation they've had with a pupil that was an honest encounter based on mutual respect and trust. Yet this is the stuff that reveals thinking, attitudes, and values, and that opens new vistas for exploration.

Conversation is a sharing process. Each participant seeks to understand the other person's point of view and also to have his own point of view understood. There are challenges not in terms of right or wrong but in terms of logical deduction, facts, additional data to be considered, and consistency. There is mutual exploration of ideas, with each person sharing insights, looking at relevant questions, and discussing related experiences and knowledge.

The teacher has a major responsibility to set an environment and climate in which discussions and conversations flow. These interchanges are not only between teacher and pupil but between pupil and pupil as well. How the teacher handles conversation has a great effect on how free children feel to think critically, to offer uncertain ideas, to pursue interesting questions, and to attempt something and fail.

The classroom material resources can offer wide opportunity for individual pursuit. But the prevailing climate will largely determine whether these materials will be explored along the ideas children have or along the ideas that children "guess" the teacher to have.

As children become involved in interesting activities, discussion can help to deepen experiences and to open new doors for exploration. Knowing when to initiate a discussion, what remarks to make, and how long to participate in the conversation takes a great deal of skill. This develops as the teacher accumulates knowledge about each child and gains experiences to assess and analyze.

A child intensely absorbed in his work may find a teacher's attempt at discussion annoying. The teacher must be sensitive to nonverbal clues as he observes a child. Timing is important. It

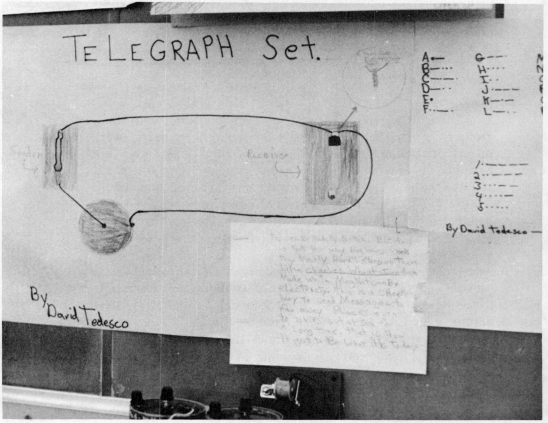

INFORMAL TEACHING IN THE OPEN CLASSROOM

may be far better to wait for a later opportunity than to move too quickly.

The discussion should be started on the basis that it can grow or can be left with very little interaction. Working alongside the child and becoming involved in the activity may be the starter. At other times a simple question like "How's it going?" or offering a new resource with the remark "This may be useful" will begin a flow of talk.

Conversation should in no way take from the child control over the learning endeavor. The teacher's positive intervention is to highlight experience, extend thinking, and share in the process of work and discovery. The child's autonomy is maintained. His personal control is strengthened as the inter-action between teacher and pupil develops the child's sense of power and extends his ability.

EXTENDING INTERESTS

Discussion can give scope to a child's interest or to a group's activity. Sometimes the teacher builds by being aware of potentials that various studies and explorations have.[1] For example, a snowstorm obviously had the attention of several children gathered to look out the window. The talk was largely focused on sledding, running in the snow, throwing snowballs, making snowmen, and so on. Noting the interest, the teacher asked if some of the children would like to go outside with pails and bring in some snow. Others were asked to prepare a space where the snow could be dumped. Pails were quickly filled, brought in, and dumped. A lively discussion ensued about how it felt, tasted, and even smelled. Someone asked, "How long before it melts?" Together the children and the teacher began to explore the possibilities of various studies and experiments that would provide answers to some of their questions. Ideas like these were developed and explored:

● Cups of snow were located in various parts of the room to observe the rate of melting. Comparisons were made. This led to a decision to check temperatures at each of the

---

[1]See pp. 71-73, Chapter 3.

locations and to graph the melting rate of snow and the temperatures found. Relationships were observed and discussed. Spin-offs began to emerge—could you build a snow clock? Would snow melt faster in the hallway? Would there be a difference between how fast the snow melted at the ceiling and at the floor?

- Various amounts of snow were melted to see how much water each amount made. A snow-to-water-ratio table was devised. Other questions were raised. Would the ratio table hold true for falling snow versus snow that had been on the ground for an hour? Was all snow of the same wetness? (Children agreed to keep a record of findings and test out snowballs during the year.) What was the relationship between the weight of the snow and the water amount?

- Words, songs, and stories related to snow became a subject of interest. A chart of "The Language of Snow" was devised listing song titles, story titles, and words that the class could recall. It was decided to extend the survey to other classes.

- The size and shape of snowflakes were investigated. Children attempted to use the microscope for a closer look. The library was checked for books that might have pictures. Snowflake patterns were cut out and hung around the room. Experimentation was begun to develop a musical rhythm of snow falling. This was interpreted in dance and finally became "The Snowflake Blues."

- Could snow be made in the classroom? An experiment was devised after much research.

- A mural showing the world of snow was made. Added questions pursued included the following: How many people live where it snows? How many people live where it doesn't? How does snow affect living conditions? Recreation? Are there diseases or illnesses related to snow?

Studies like those described began as a casual interest largely related to recreation. The teacher made the difference. Resources quickly assembled contributed to getting the children involved in direct experience. Beginning questions, ideas, and suggestions from the teacher helped to make children aware of the many possibilities for study and investigations. Discussions and added resources of records, books, and color slides gave new dimensions and helped children to continue studies that led to new question. Recordings, exhibits, murals, and children's writings displayed around the room communicated findings and give the teacher opportunities for talking with the class and individuals about their work.

Teachers do not need to wait for a snowstorm, or other happenings, to catch children's interest in order to move. The classroom environment can be constructed to help. An "investigative table" is one way. Here a frequently changing assortment of "junk," broken appliances, and throwaway items can be displayed. But again the teacher, aware of the possibilities of investigations, can make the difference between a once-over-fingering-of-objects by children or the development of exciting studies.

- A broken electric clock led a group into a whole study of clocks. Water clocks, sand clocks, and sun clocks were devised and tested. A mural showed the historical development of clocks. (Here books found by the teacher initially set the stage.) A classroom day without clocks was tried. Hunger in relation to time was observed. (With the consent of the teacher, and without the class's knowledge, a committee moved the classroom clock ahead an hour one day and back an hour another day. Interviews with classmates regarding hunger were conducted during the week—on days when the clock was accurate as well as on days when it had been changed.) Cost of clocks, famous clocks, the clock industry, and the different time zones were other thrusts.

- An assortment of junk helped some children get started making a model. At first the model was a free-form, artistic endeavor. A chance remark by one of the pupils, "It looks like a moon city," gave the teacher a clue for conversation. As the talk developed questions began to arise—how would the temperature on the moon affect the kind of buildings needed? What about wind? Rain? Gravity? The kind of land? The teacher scurried to get materials—magazine pictures, newspaper stories of a few months and years ago (newspapers maintain a library that can be used—sometimes copies are available or can be made of relevant stories), and books helped to keep the interest alive and foster its growth. Children decided to write to their congressmen for any government printed materials. NASA was contacted. Local architects were interviewed for their views on what buildings on the moon would look like. The project grew and became an exciting exhibit, "Our Moon City." Drawings, sketches, results of interviews, replies to letters, models, and factual findings were all part of the display. And spin-offs were developing as other children watched the exhibit grow—What would people do on the moon? What kind of music would develop? How would first dwellers feel? Would a study of how first dwellers in America, in Mexico, in Europe felt provide clues? What about dress on the moon? What have been the effects of moon exploration on life here on earth—in medicine, in fashion, in daily living, and so on?

A table of "junk" provided the start. The children's initial curiosity and first attempts at doing something were beginning points. The teacher, sensitive to developments, helped the children to identify their interests and to expand the beginning activity.

Caution is exerted so that whatever develops reflects the children's ideas and not teacher direction. Moving too quickly can easily break the fragile thread of first interests. And yet waiting too long can cause an opportunity to be missed. The teacher helps by enlarging conversation and by building on children's remarks.

Possible resources are identified. Suggestions stemming from the children's talk are made. Questions are raised. Clarification of ideas is attempted. All in all, the teacher works to help the children freely set tentative directions for further explorations.

DEEPENING CHILDREN'S LEARNING

Setting the study or investigation is obviously a first priority. How a teacher functions in the total process of deepening learning and bringing it to the conscious level is a further concern.

Studies start from different points. For some children an interest is rather sharp and clear. For others there is only an apparent random activity. Doodling, a monotonous repetition of drawing an object over and over, wandering around the room fingering first one thing and then another, trying for a few minutes to do something and then changing to something else—it's as though the child is stuck and doesn't know how to change gears. It may be that he doesn't even realize what he is doing. It's the kind of behavior that need not be stopped from the standpoint of interference of others, physical harm, or destruction of property. Rather the teacher is aware that even this type of behavior as well as the kind related to a well-defined interest can, with positive teacher intervention, become the basis for extended work.

A child's repetitious drawing of a motorcycle can be used as a starting point to describe when and how the teacher intervenes in positive ways. A flow chart of the teacher's work and the developing study illustrates key processes:

Teacher Observes:

THE ACTIVITY

John is drawing pictures of motorcycles. The pictures seemingly are the same—size varies somewhat but the type of cycle does not. John appears to be in a repetitious rut—he's absorbed, he's quiet, but so far the activity has led nowhere.

Teacher Initiates Conversation:

TALKING TOGETHER

The teacher attempts to determine the child's interest and purpose in order to support. Questions like these help to gather data:

"Tell me about what you're doing."
"How's it going?"
"What made you decide to draw motorcycles?"

Responses to initial starter questions provide direction for the conversation. The development of the talk builds upon the child's comments and thought. The teacher attempts to maintain openness so that possible next steps can emerge.

Teacher-Pupil Develop Next Steps:

EXTENDING THE ACTIVITY—
USING OTHER EXPRESSIVE FORMS

The teacher-pupil talk provides clues as to possible further steps. Expressing the interest, concern, or tentative idea through another activity form may help to strengthen the child's purpose or provide the child with additional insight as to what he is trying to do, to accomplish, or to explore. Other possible activities include—

—Making a model of a motorcycle (clay or wood).
—Making a recording of sounds of various motorcycles at various speeds.
—Visiting stores to see motorcycles.
—Looking at catalogues or magazines to find out about different kinds of motorcycles, costs, and so on.
—Collecting pictures of motorcycles.
—Writing stories to accompany motorcycle drawings.
—Preparing an exhibit "all about motorcycles."
—Interviewing motorcycle owners, other children, teachers.
—Making a traffic count of motorcycles during a day, a week, at home, at school, and so on.
—Organizing a club for all who may be interested in motorcycles.
—Doing rubbings of motorcycle tires.
—Making castings of motorcycle tracks.

Teacher-Pupil Dialogue; Teacher Enlarges and Deepens Scope of Study:

DEVELOPING THE STUDY—
DEEPENING THE EXPERIENCE

Teacher and pupil continue their dialogue looking at the extended activity to see what interests the child. Tentative questions to explore emerge. The framework of a study develops.

Teacher draws upon knowledge of tools, processes, and techniques as well as content of disciplines to frame questions and to offer guidance for investigation. The teacher thinks in parallel lines for each discipline: What are the questions? How does the investigator work? In this way "All About Motorcycles" can be related to

History.	Physics.	Music.
Geography.	Physiology.	Geology.
Economics.	Astrology.	↓
Psychology.	Mathematics.	
Sociology.	Literature.	Anthropology.

Teacher Acts to Bring Learning to Conscious Level:

DEVELOPING CONSCIOUS VERBAL LEARNING

The teacher provides and expands language.
> The teacher adds to the child's experience by providing terminology and language to help the child to talk about what he's doing. The input of language follows, *rather than precedes*, the understanding or conceptualization.

The teacher helps to link experiences.
> Current experience is linked to previous learnings to clinch developments and to assist in the further analysis and interpretation of findings.

The teacher does direct teaching.
> Direct teaching at the point of need is provided. This may be in the area of skills, new processes, new techniques, or further refinements of previous learnings.

The Teacher Monitors the Development of the Study:

MONITORING

The teacher serves as a monitor during the study to see that the child considers

1. Planning and results.
2. Actions and feelings.
3. Learnings and goals.
4. Accomplishments and unanswered questions.

The focus is on self-assessment and evaluation.
The pupil takes primary responsibility.

A focus on each of these phases may help to clarify the teacher's role and provide a basis for why the teacher intervenes. By a tracing of the development of an activity through to its evolvement as an in-depth study, various elements of the teacher's role can be seen in relationship. It should be obvious that such a progression does not always occur, not is it necessary. The teacher may join in at middle stages or later stages, having missed earlier developments. With a classroom full of children, it's frequently not possible to be at beginning points for each child as he moves into deeper learning experiences. Nevertheless, an understanding of key role elements, their relationships and functions, and the underlying rationale can help the teacher to function in meaningful ways in the classroom. This is the focus of the description of each of the phases as the teacher moves to invest an activity with significant learning.

The activity is an exploration stage, a time of "mucking around" when one is attempting to settle on a task. Children as well as adults go through periods when energy is seemingly scattered over a variety of very short-term engagements or focused on repetitious meanderings. Teachers may recognize for themselves that on some weekends they had feelings of great accomplishment, that their activities were purposeful, and that

INFORMAL TEACHING IN THE OPEN CLASSROOM

time passed by in meaningful and satisfying ways. Whereas there are other weekends when first one thing and then another was attempted and nothing got finished, nor was there a focusing of energy toward any one purposeful activity. It was a hit-and-miss affair. Seemingly they couldn't find a project to explore or to concentrate on in depth.

Although these periods can be frustrating they are apparently needed and useful in the nature of self-directed activity. Certainly they can be expected—a part of the process of determining for one's self how and on what to expend energy. Positive intervention, however, by another person can help the individual to discover purpose, to clarify interest, and to make a decision on a focus of attention.

Talking together helps the child to move from seemingly random or scattered activity toward a study or investigation. In the talking-together process the teacher makes several professional judgments based on available data.

1. When to initiate the talk? Early intervention by the teacher can be unsettling and actually delay the meaningful development of a study. Children do need time to explore. "Wasting time" is frequently preliminary to long-term productive work. An intervention too quickly made by the teacher can result in short-term work or a project started but never finished. Better timing results if the teacher observes the pupil, matches the observation with knowledge about the pupil, and assesses the impact of the general classroom activity upon the particular pupil. These become the components of decision making, not as a detailed prolonged study but as factors to consider in making the professional judgment of when to act.

2. How to initiate the talk? The handle for beginning talk with the child relates to what he appears to be doing but with an openness that allows the unexpected response. "I see you're interested in motorcycles" can be an erroneous assumption. There may be no interest—in fact the child may hardly be aware of the object he is drawing. The teacher's question or statement must express the feeling that "I'm interested, I care about what you're doing" while making no assumption or judgment about the activity. And still further the initial thrust should be such that the child who's not yet ready or

for some reason is unwilling to focus on conversation at the moment can feel free to halt the beginning conversation temporarily.

The purpose of the teacher's positive intervention is to be of help to the child in clarifying his interest, finding a direction for further action, and firming up his purpose. The teacher does not attempt to guide or to manipulate the child subtly toward the teacher's own end. Rather the talk is an honest exhange that may be useful to the child.

Activities are stopped if they are physically harmful to the child, if they are destructive of property, or if they infringe on the rights of others. Activities may be relocated to a more suitable place. For example, flying a paper airplane may be inappropriate in the classroom because of possible danger to others, so the project may be relocated, perhaps to a corridor or outside, because of the potential it has for challenging studies. But the activity engaged in by the child is not given purpose by the teacher nor stopped because of some teacher constraint. The teacher seeks to be a resource to the child, to help him clarify his purpose and interest.

Extending the activity is a frequent outcome of the teacher-pupil talk. At initial stages of exploration the pupil is not yet fixed on what he really wants to do or how. There may be only a spark. The conversation helps to provide further ideas to keep the spark alive. At this stage another activity may be better than to move too quickly into a research process or an investigation. Various activities are suggested to build upon what has been done. These help

- To maintain the beginning interest or focused attention.

- To provide additional data to the teacher about what the interest and purpose is.

- To help the child "firm up" possible directions by trying out alternative expressive modes.

- To provide time for the teacher to gather possible useful resources and tools.

Basically, the intent is to explore in another way the initial random or repetitious activity. With this additional work a study or investigation may emerge that is interesting to the child and that expands learning.

Setting the study and developing its dimensions flow from the activity stage as the teacher and the pupil talk together. Of course the teacher must be aware that studies and investigations do not always result at this point. The child may have attempted another activity somehow related to his first actions of drawing motorcycles only to discover that there is nothing that interests him about motorcycles or related ideas. There is no forcing of "setting a study." The teacher functions as a help in clarifying interests and serves as a resource for possible study ideas. The child makes the decision. Consequently if the activities attempted do not suggest anything of particular interest to the child, he probably resumes his exploration and the process starts afresh.

Many times, though, questions and experiences to explore begin to take shape as the child moves from the apparent random activity toward a more focused activity based on some part of the initial exercise. The teacher and pupil, in talking about these new developments, may begin to formulate a tentative study—an investigation that will explore a variety of questions and seek to bring together different kinds of data for analysis and interpretation.

The teacher's knowledge about the tools, techniques, and processes as well as the general body of content of the various disciplines is an important resource. This basic knowledge stimulates the teacher to think of possible questions to explore and possible ways of moving. For example, if finding out about motorcycles does become the beginning point for a study, the teacher can offer guidelines and possible directions for study by thinking about motorcycles and history, physics, literature, psychology, geography, economics, mathematics, sociology, health, and so on. Working together the pupil and the teacher gradually expand the study and build questions to explore that serve as a groundwork for the development of concepts, principles, understandings, and generalizations. At this stage activity becomes invested with potential for significant in-depth learning that develops as the child continues his exploration.

Developing conscious verbal learning is an ongoing process during the course of the study. Basically the teacher functions in three very important ways. These are overlapping functions interwoven during the total process of experience. Nevertheless, to consider each separately may help to clarify the nature of each.

1. *Fostering Language Growth.* Experiences and understandings become the bases for the use and need of language. The teacher provides appropriate terms and language to help the pupil talk about what he is doing. However, terminology and labels are introduced as outcomes of the experience and the child's understanding. To introduce language too early can impede the development of a full understanding. Children need to have the opportunity of working out things without being hampered by language. Language growth for the child is more solidly built upon experience. There needs to be a genuine use of language rather than rote verbalism. If terms and labels are learned without an understanding of what is really meant, development at later stages is hampered not only in terms of knowledge but in terms of further clarification and extension of learning as well. Accurate language appropriate to the level of understanding helps the child move to further thinking. It is possible that language introduced at the right time can do much to help the child observe greater detail and relationships, resulting in abstractions and generalizations.

   Discovery learning is, of course, related to understanding rather than language as a tool. It is absurd to expect children to discover terminology and appropriate language to describe results. The teacher, knowing the language, does not withhold it but rather contributes this as a resource to be used by the child.

2. *Linking Experiences.* An experience hooked onto a previous one in some way helps to shape the dimension of the experience and make it more meaningful within the child's own structuring of learning. The teacher plays a vital role in this hooking-up process. It is not only the simple remembering of this in relation to something previous but, more important, the linking of key elements and factors of

experiences. The attempt is to bring to a conscious level similar relationships and results. Questions such as the following help in this process—

—What happens when you do this?
—What would happen if you change this?
—How do you explain what happens?
—Do you always get the same results?
—Would the same thing happen if someone else did the same thing?

The teacher's role in drawing attention to relevant elements of experiences helps the child build bridges between the old and the new so that restructuring of thinking grows. Answers to such questions as these provide essential information for the formulation of generalizations and development of concepts.

3. *Direct Teaching.* Direct teaching does occur in the open informal classroom. Sometimes it is to an individual child. At other times it is to a small group. But always it is timed to fit the children's willingness and ability to learn. Direct teaching is a resource available to the children when needed, as particular stoppages or blocks to further learning are met.

The teacher, through training, education, maturity, and experience, does have expertise to offer. There are the multitude of observations made of children's struggles, explorations, and accomplishments. There is knowledge of the structure, tools, and content of disciplines. And there is knowledge of multiple approaches that can be tried experimentally in seeking a solution, an answer, an insight, or understanding. This is the professional knowledge and skill that the teacher brings to children.

Direct teaching is a positive intervention when it's tied to children's interests and needs. It is first and foremost a relationship, not, the passing on of something to someone. The teacher meshes personal knowledge of the child's development and the structural elements of what is to be learned. This knitting together of the natural learning rhythm and pattern of the child and appropriate tasks contributes to orderly thinking and problem-solving power for the child with which he can meet future learning needs.

Direct teaching is couched in terms of building the child's self-power, not in terms of taking away or enhancing teacher control. That each child must learn for himself and no one can learn for him is not just a statement to bandy about. It must be the basis for direct teaching. And it becomes so when instruction is personalized, is built upon children's choice, and is designed to give power to the learner.

Monitoring is a reminding function, calling attention to previously made commitments and decisions. The teacher role is to see that the child is thinking about what he is doing and is thinking ahead. There is an expectation that pupils will make plans and follow the plans made. Changes in plans are perfectly acceptable when made on the basis of careful thought, not momentary whims and impulses. Monitoring focuses on the processes involved, that is, on the consideration given to the development of criteria and to the follow-through. Does the plan of evaluation include a look at a variety of areas and provide reasonable ways to gather data? Is evaluation being implemented according to thoughtful decisions?

To build data for future planning, evaluation, and consideration, as well as for study outcomes, recording is expected. Reminding children about recording data and providing help and guidance related to useful types of recording are part of the monitoring process.

Monitoring flows from observation. The intent is to strengthen pupil responsibility and rational behaving. It must not deteriorate into constant checking or regimentation. Monitoring should emphasize pupil control, not teacher control. Pupil power in learning is built when actions stem from thoughtful plans carried out in effective ways. Monitoring provides adult guidance emphasizing order in freedom.

THE TEACHER'S WORK DAY

Finding time to implement fully the personal interactions of informal teaching is always a problem. Organizing teacher time at initial stages can help in the process of developing various role facets. As experience is gained, the teacher's time

INFORMAL TEACHING IN THE OPEN CLASSROOM

schedule becomes much more fluid and flexible. But even then it's helpful to take an occasional look at how classroom time is spent.

To organize the work day the teacher might look at six broad categories of work and the kind of personal interactions and group dynamics involved in each. Functionally, the teacher could categorize teaching actions in these ways:

● Individual conferencing.

● Small group teaching.

● Committee/project consultation and conferencing.

● Observation.

● Large group work.

● Discussion and seminar participation.

A further look at each of these in terms of typical examples, discussion of salient points to keep in mind as the teacher works in this way, and some general pointers regarding implementation can be helpful. The teacher should recognize that the individual development of ways of working grows not only from an understanding of the nature of informal teaching but, very importantly, from the application of efforts within the specific classroom context—the children involved as well as other innumerable factors influencing the classroom. Informal teaching is flexible, not rigid. It is timed in relation to the child to be a resource available to him at the point of his need. With this frame of reference and with cautions outlined, a discussion of each way of working is presented to clarify and broaden the meaning involved.

Individual Conference Time

Individual conferencing is in many ways the heart of informal teaching. It is a period of intense interaction between the learner and the teacher. It is a personal involvement between two people working together in a cooperative, give-and-take relationship that builds on the feelings of equality and mutual concern. The individual conference draws upon the resources of both parties to focus on a recognized interest, need, or problem. Outcomes are mutually satisfying and more frequently a progression toward growth rather than quick remedies or imposed solutions.

Conference time is sometimes arranged by the pupil, sometimes scheduled by the teacher. At initial stages of the changeover to informal teaching the teacher may schedule individual conferences to introduce and to develop a new pattern of working. As children become more familiar with the intent and focus of conference time, the teacher moves to establish the climate and procedures whereby the pupils themselves can initiate conferences. One simple technique that has worked is that of having pupils wanting a conference to list their names on the chalkboard. The teacher works hard to confer with these children if at all possible during the day in order to encourage moves in this direction. Eventually the teacher anticipates conference time to include both pupil-initiated and teacher-initiated conferences. The teacher will find it meaningful to initiate conferences occasionally. Consequently the teacher does not "hold back" but is an active participant in classroom living and learning, as is the child.

The frequency of conferences and the length of time for each can vary a great deal. There are no set schedules nor rigid time requirements. However, some guidelines can help the teacher develop the pattern and rhythm most meaningful to the individual child. At first, conferences tend to be frequent. For the young child, a couple of conferences a day may be needed. Eventually this may decrease to once a day or even every other day. For the older child once a day at the beginning may change to two or three times a week at later stages. It should be obvious that the individual conference is not the only time there is personal contact between the teacher and the pupil. During the day there will be many quick interactions, as the teacher supports the child in his work, asks questions, or offers suggestions. These pupil-teacher interactions, although valuable, do not replace the need for conferences.

Conference time need not be lengthy. Three- to five-minute conferences (sometimes even shorter) for young children

INFORMAL TEACHING IN THE OPEN CLASSROOM

and perhaps' as long as seven minutes for older children are general guidelines. Longer conferences have the disadvantages of tying up the teacher and making it difficult for other children to get help. But, more importantly, an effective conference can "cover" only so much ground in terms of helping the pupil to plot the next steps or to carry out agreed-upon decisions. More frequent short conferences are probably preferable to long conferences. And, of course, a simple calculation of the total available time for conferences and the number of children involved will show that the conference must be focused and intense rather than a "chit-chat" session.

Whether the child or the teacher initiates the conference, it's desirable to have the interaction focused to make it most meaningful. The conference is not the only point of contact. If it is to contribute the most to the whole range of teacher functioning, then some thought should be given to its design for maximum contribution. The individual conference includes interaction:

- To plan for next steps.

- To review records and previously established goals and directions.

- To identify resource needs, sources, and uses.

- To diagnose problems.

- To foster personal sharing.

- To "teach" specific things recognized as needs by the pupil and not commonly shared by other pupils.

- To seek specific help, guidance, or another viewpoint.

- To solidify or add new dimensions to thinking.

- To explore mutual concerns.

In these and other ways, the teacher and the pupil make use of conference time for learning growth and development.

Both are aware of the intended significance and in-depth exploration and work to make it mutually satisfying. The teacher is particularly cognizant of the personal and intense nature of conference time and seeks to establish a recognition on the part of all pupils in the class that one does not interrupt this personal exchange. Pupils, realizing that the time will be short and that there will be an opportunity for quick questions at the end of one conference before a new one is started, not only learn to wait but to appreciate the courtesy of noninterruption when they are the ones talking with the teacher.

Small Group Teaching

There are times for direct teaching. What makes the difference for learning, though, is whether this teaching is connected to intrinsic learning.[2] The teacher does have expertise to offer. It's the timing, the motivation (pupil versus teacher), and the need (pupil versus "coverage") that make significant differences. Within this context, direct teaching can be termed not only efficient but practical. Efficiency and practicality are seen from the point of view of helping pupils learn, not coverage of material.

This direct teaching is a resource. It may indeed be an offering designed by the teacher and scheduled because of what the teacher has observed and learned from personal interactions. But who participates is a decision made by individual pupils as each considers his needs, plans, and progress. Of course, a poor decision may be made and this may become a focus for an individual conference. Nevertheless, if pupils are to grow in the ability to solve problems, decisions on how and when to use the resources offered is an area where experiencing can help in the development of learning strength.

Again, however, at initial stages of changeover the teacher may need to build guidelines to facilitate pupil growth and at least attempt to ensure rational thinking about the decision to

---

[2]See Jeannette Veatch's discussion, "Some Thoughts on Direct Teaching," in her book, *For the Love of Teaching* (Encino, Calif.: The International Center for Educational Development, Ventura Boulevard, 1973).

be made. It's not unreasonable to ask a pupil to spend five minutes or so at a session before the decision is made. This can help clarify what will happen, the intent, and possible developments that offer additional data to the pupil as he considers whether the session will be a resource or not. Another possibility is to encourage pupils to design their own solutions and if these don't work, then to try the planned session. (There may be sessions designed to help pupils do this or attention focused on this during the conference period or the group planning period.) And at times, because of a strong feeling the teacher has, a pupil may even be required to participate. But the teacher clearly recognizes that the direct teaching session is intended as a resource open to pupil decision-making as to its use.

Small group teaching takes many forms and is not limited to the one or two types commonly noted in the conventional classroom. The purposes vary; the so-called content includes a variety of thrusts; and even the technique and procedures, although labeled "teaching," range considerably. Possible small group sessions may emerge from situations or be focused on areas such as these:

- Several children want to learn to operate the movie projector. A group session is designed for instruction.

- Three or four children seem to be disruptive influences in the classroom. The group is called together. The problem is outlined. Discussion ensues. Personal programs for working in ways that don't interfere with others are developed. These are tested. Later sessions focus on developments, the alterations needed, and future steps.

- Individual planning is difficult for some children. A session or sessions is designed to help focus on guideline questions to consider, various factors to think about, and possible steps to take.

- Tom, Mary, Sue, and Raphael have been reading material that has some broad relationships. They are asked to come together to share their reading and to look into the possibility of next steps, working as a group.

- The teacher has made an exciting trip abroad collecting various materials including slides. A session is designed to share the experience with children who may have an interest.

- Several children seem to be having a reading difficulty that the teacher thinks could be helped by focus on a particular skill. A skill-teaching lesson is devised and offered.

Small group teaching can have a variety of focal points. The teacher is active in organizing and offering these resources. Knowledge about a discipline, processes of learning, and teaching methods are combined to offer a teaching help for children working in the informal open classroom.

Committee/Project Consultation and Conferencing

Children do work in groups as well as individually in the open classroom. At initial stages of development a common observation is that nearly all of the pupil's day is spent in individual work, alongside other children but not in cooperation with others. Perhaps this is a natural step teachers take—the jump from large group teaching to individual pupil pursuits. The latter is frequently focused on the same material as previously, with the teacher now moving toward individual teaching. This becomes an impossible task, however, as the teacher soon learns. Formal class teaching replaced by formal individual teaching or formal individual teaching done in an informal way is not the change demanded by the open classroom rationale.

Group work in the nature of projects, committee investigations, or development of studies is important. Organizing these may initially require the teacher to bring possible groups together, to offer suggestions during planning time, to develop ideas from small group teaching sessions, or to work in some other way. Certainly such work is to be encouraged and supported.

Part of the teacher's day is spent working with such groups. In some cases the committee schedules the meeting time, which the teacher notes on his master teaching resource

INFORMAL TEACHING IN THE OPEN CLASSROOM

schedule for the day. At other times the teacher schedules a meeting of the groups. Because the teacher serves as a contributing member of each group he joins in the deliberations and work of the group at informal times as well as at the specifically scheduled times.

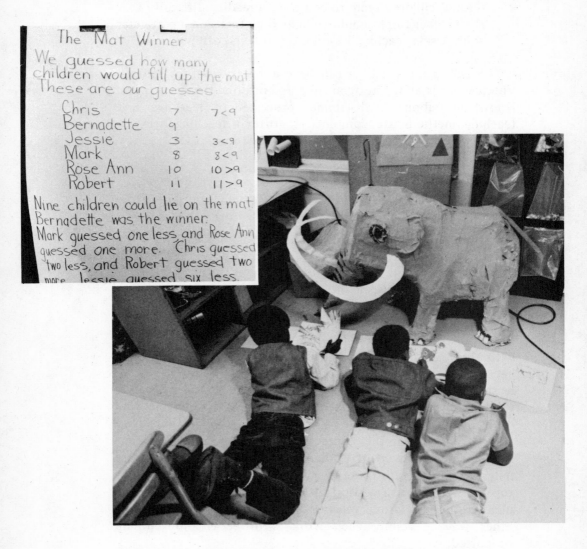

The Mat Winner

We guessed how many children would fill up the mat. These are our guesses.

Chris	7	7 < 9
Bernadette	9	
Jessie	3	3 < 9
Mark	8	8 < 9
Rose Ann	10	10 > 9
Robert	11	11 > 9

Nine children could lie on the mat. Bernadette was the winner. Mark guessed one less, and Rose Ann guessed one more. Chris guessed two less, and Robert guessed two more. Jessie guessed six less.

How the teacher functions can range widely. At times the role is predominantly one of exploring questions: Where are you? How's it going? What are your tentative findings? What are the next steps? Have you considered this? Other actions may include checking on resource needs and arranging to get needed materials. The teacher may make notes regarding progress, and developments to watch for or focus on ways of sharing the committee's effort beyond the classroom, such as at PTA night or for general school use. Some input may relate to how the committee is functioning and helping the group clarify roles, organization, or management procedures. In these and other ways the teacher strengthens group work and helps it to develop. Committee work frequently results in exhibits, murals, reports, models, or other products that stimulate and expand children's interests. Group resources such as these contribute immeasurably to the richness of the open classroom environment.

Observation

Teaching is a demanding profession. Each child is different. The effective teacher must know not only about children's growth, development, and learning but about the individual child. The general knowledge, understandings, and principles are only starting points. Positive teacher action with any one child is built upon specific insight into and knowledge of that child. These change, grow, develop, and take shape as the teacher observes and works with the child. Thought must be given not only to the analysis and interpretation of the data amassed but also to obtaining new data to broaden the picture constantly. It is an ever-evolving task and a constant role of the effective teacher.

Much of the growing understanding teachers have about pupils comes about in the minute-by-minute, hour-by-hour work with children. But a planned time, a time established with learning about children as its focus, can be most important. It's not unreasonable for the teacher to schedule this in his working day. Such a procedure is especially useful as teachers make the move to develop the functioning open classroom. If conventional teaching has been the style, then the teacher may discover he knows little about individual children in terms of their hopes, fears, interests, needs, learning styles, hobbies, thinking patterns, and so on. At first as well as later these factors can become the basis of specific observation, interaction times. For example, today from 10:00-10:15 I'll

- Observe the behaviors of children when they are reading.

- Note the questions children ask.

- Look at the materials children are actually using.

- Talk with five children about what they did after school yesterday.

- Review children's art work in terms of interests, feelings, thinking.

- Check the noises of learning.

- Observe who is working with whom and the nature of the involvement.

These are only some of the ways the teacher uses this time to gather data, to focus on the meaning involved, and to increase insight into and understanding of the children with whom he works. Such a time and such a function make an important contribution to informal teaching that has personal learning as a core feature. The teacher acts as a scientific investigator, a student of child growth and development, and a researcher in the psychology of learning. This professional knowledge is not for prescription purposes but for the humane purpose of being an effective adult in the personal interacting relationship with each child and his learning.

The time is established so the class understands its importance and will function in noninterruptive ways when the teacher is so engaged. The time can occasionally be used for other important functions—catching up on teacher records, contacting individual pupils as the teacher meanders around the classroom, and even "teacher thinking." It is a time when the teacher attempts to see, to hear, to feel the class as an objective observer. From this the teacher devises and tests the ever-increasing dimensions of the role of informal teaching for the children involved.

Large Group Work

There are appropriate times and functions for large group or whole class work. The extent does diminish considerably as compared with conventional teaching. But the whole class is, in effect, the immediate community to which loyalties and feelings of belonging are appropriate. And some activities and experiences require large groups to be effectively experienced. For example, many music activities, physical education activities, and games need the participation of many children. There are other activities in which numbers can be large or small and either is acceptable, e.g., viewing a film, listening to a recording, or watching a game.

There are other occasions when it's well to start with the total group even though the latter part of the activity may involve a smaller number. One example is planning. The whole class may focus on planning at the beginning of the day. By the same token the end of the day may focus on assessment and evaluation. Although each individual is to develop his own plan or evaluate his work, the teacher may well initiate the activity by giving some general ideas for resources and things to consider or by asking a few children to contribute their thoughts as a stimulus and a guide to others. What begins as total group work eventually becomes individual responses. But the togetherness in terms of focus does serve a useful purpose.

"Town meetings" related to class problems or interests are also useful as large group experiences. These sometimes start with an individual's or a small group's giving attention to some facet of group life and wanting to involve the whole class. Certainly there are problems that must be solved and interests to be developed in common if outcomes are to be effective, useful, or desirable.

One class uses the technique of class meetings daily. The agenda for these meetings comes from a chalkboard listing of concerns, questions, or comments. Each pupil during the day is free to make any notation. He writes his name as the person concerned. The class meeting, chaired by a different pupil elected each week, moves through the agenda. The pupil who has written each item, clarifies it for the class. A discussion is held and appropriate action taken, the next item is taken up, and so on. Any items not covered are carried over to the next day at the top of the list. In this way the class thinks through a variety of concerns. The teacher, like the pupils, is free to add his items as well.

Large groups or the whole class is involved for a variety of purposes. But seldom is this for "teaching." In fact, the teacher should constantly be on guard against doing something with the whole class in order "to save time" or for "efficiency" purposes. Seldom are these legitimate reasons for whole class activity. Rather the questions "Is this something useful to foster the spirit of community? something that requires whole class attention? or something that needs large numbers for development?" are far more basic to consider when whole class involvement is contemplated.

Discussion and Seminar Participation

Frequent discussions help increase the quality of experiences for children. Informal talk among children occurring regularly and spontaneously does much, but group discussions that are semiorganized can add still another dimension. The teacher plays a significant role, helping to clarify ideas, synthesizing findings, and developing additional explorations. Some discussions will move into the area of making judgments or inferences. Generalizations may be hypothesized and additional testing methods frequently emerge. In these and other ways, discussions help bring learnings to the conscious level, add new directions to interests, and deepen and enrich the active experience.

The teacher may frequently take the lead in arranging discussion groups. Some groups will cut across various individual studies and investigations. The focus may be to look at the process used to investigate certain things. For example, one or two students may be trying to find out about student attitudes toward drug usage. Another pupil may be working on a neighborhood survey related to community history. Still another is involved in finding out student preferences for singing groups. The teacher, seeing the potential for group discussion, invites the children involved to get together to analyze the techniques involved in gathering data through surveys. The problem of sampling techniques, ideas for questions, and ways of testing procedures may become part of the discussion. The focus or "starting-together" point is on the process of investigation. How it develops and what emerges from the group discussion depend on a variety of elements. But unless the teacher sees the potential, the group might miss out on an experience that could lead in a variety of enriching directions. A resource is added to the environment through positive teacher action.

The focal points for group discussions are numerous. The teacher can form a group by asking children making a study of early Indians to come together with those who are studying the people of Japan. Common elements include contrasting and comparing similarities, differences, and patterns of life for man in different parts of the world. Other groups may be formed to pool knowledge about a topic that has been individually investigated. Other discussions may be in the form of "rap" sessions in which participants talk about how they feel, what they like or don't like, conditions of schooling, possible improvements, and so on. It's a time for an honest exchange of viewpoints and an attempt to develop insights and understandings that can lead to improvement, better conditions, and learning growth.

The discussion seminar is a valuable part of the teacher's daily work. Part of his role relates to organizing groups, facilitating individuals' getting together, and calling attention to common interests that may lead to group work. Another part of the role relates to the teacher at work within the group, participating and contributing to the discussion but avoiding leading or directing it. Discussions in the open classroom are recognized as important and valuable experiences to be developed.

The Teacher's Schedule

As the teacher functions in the ways discribed, the question arises as to how much time should be spent and when. There are no hard and fast rules, but beginning guidelines can help. Such guidelines are only to stimulate thinking so that the teacher plans how time is to be spent rather than being a slave to happenings.

Ideas to consider include such things as the following:

1. The major part of the time will be spent in individual conferences—perhaps 50 to 60 per cent of the day. If it is to be the heart, then it takes a major share of time.
2. Observation time—perhaps 15 to 20 minutes, once a day or split between two periods—probably is a realistic allotment. If some allotment isn't made, then it's likely that this important function will be neglected. And to neglect it could seriously handicap the teacher in terms of fostering personal learning for each child.
3. Time devoted to large group teaching will be minimal. But some days will include more time for it than others because of special activities.
4. The balance of the day (still a healthy percentage) is probably split between small group teaching, committee and project consultations, and discussion sessions with groups.

To develop the working pattern the teacher may find it helpful to post a general schedule of how he plans to spend his day. The schedule, not a rigid plan but flexible, can be helpful to children as they plan their work. A schedule might look like this:

Teacher's Schedule

9:00-9:20.	Assisting with learning plans.
9:20-10:30.	Individual conferences.
10:30-11:00.	Physical education.
11:00-11:45.	Small group instruction (see master resource plan).
11:45-12:30.	Lunch.
12:30-1:15.	Individual conferences.
1:15-1:30.	Observation.
1:30-2:45.	Discussion groups and committee consultations.
2:45-3:00.	Clean up, evaluation session.

Scheduling at the early stages of developing the open classroom helps the teacher maintain control over a new way of working while trying to develop positive teacher intervention. By no means is it suggested that scheduling is essential. Eventually the teacher's work day will flow naturally as he acts in response to needs and interests and also as a positive force. Nevertheless, the teacher should take occasional stock of how time is spent in order to know what adjustments may be needed if his action is to continue to be effective.

CHAPTER 5

Using Records

The diversity of individual work patterns and activities in the informal open classroom immediately raises the question, "How does the teacher keep track of what's going on?" The concern is to know not only about the individual child but to maintain a general picture about the class as a whole. Additional questions include "Who keeps the records?" and "What kinds of records?" and "How to find time for this seemingly additional task?"

"Keeping track" is only one dimension of using records. They can be practical tools with a variety of purposes and uses. Some records help pupils clarify and define plans for action. Analysis of recorded information may be a basis for growth in thinking and gaining additional insights into solving problems. Through records a pattern of work becomes more visible. Practices that may be rather one-sided or limited in terms of successful problem-solving can be identified and changed.

At times a record may be useful to help a child solve a particular problem or clear up a difficulty. Possibilities for next steps in learning emerge as records are reviewed. This information provides valuable data for conferencing with the pupil and the parent. The recommendations, whether made by the pupil, the parent, or the teacher can be based on fact. Information on class projects, interests, committee work all help to alert teachers and pupils to possible directions for exploration and investigation. As new projects get under way possible ideas for new studies become clearer. Resources can be collected and made available to build on the edges of learning.

Records carefully devised and well used add much to the success of informal teaching in the open classroom. The questions of who keeps what records and for what purposes need thoughtful attention.

TEACHER RECORDS

Teachers can easily get bogged down with records. There is a common urge to plunge into record keeping as conventional practices give way to informal teaching methods. "How will I know what the children are doing?" becomes a common concern. The familiar guideposts of assignments made, books covered, time alloted to various subjects in a timetabled day are gone. Of course what we fail to realize is that these provided little information about what pupils were thinking or learning; these were only signs of requirements and what was covered by the teacher. Nevertheless, the concern to be informed, to gain greater insight into the growth and development of each individual is legitimate and some system of recording data can be useful.

What records and how many are questions not easily answered. At the transition stages certain records will be more useful than at later stages. Guidelines such as these may be helpful:

- *Develop an experimental attitude.* Ask "What do I really want (need) to know?" Devise a record to get the information. Try it out for a few days. Seriously look at it in terms of the information obtained, the time required, and the adjusted value placed on the results. Think about possible shortcuts. *Revise and retest.*

- *Consider whether you need the same information about all children.* Ask "What do I really need to know most about

Martha, Tom, Henry, Dana?" Devise a record system that allows you to get different information about different children at different times.

- *Check what you're doing to see if there is a continued need for doing what you started.* Think of another way of getting the information—use of class records, review of pupil-kept records, or periodic class discussions.

Some teachers devise records to provide a general overview of the class (Sample 1).[1] The teacher notes one or two observations, a phrase or a word about each child working in several areas during a two-week period. At initial stages, the comments might be books being read, problems being worked on, or experiments being carried out. A variation of this form is seen in Sample 2. Here the familiar subject divisions are gone and the comments may be about anything of importance. To supplement this form and to focus observation on a particular area, the teacher may each week use a form for observation in a subject area. This might be a check list related to general skills as shown in Sample 3 or a more general form related to a specific development in a subject area, such as shown in Samples 4 and 5. Because the form is changed weekly, the teacher begins over a period of time to amass data not only in several specific areas for each child but also in general ways of working through the use of the form shown in Sample 2.

Although at intitial stages the teacher may feel lost because he isn't as aware of what's going on as he felt he used to be, this does change with time. Invariably, teachers report an increased knowledge and understanding of individual children's growth and development as they work in the open classroom. Records seem to diminish and the teacher's senses seem to be ever sharper in obtaining valuable data through observing children and talking to them about what they're doing and thinking.

Recording at this point frequently is in anecdotal form of actual pupil behavior within a specific context. The teacher may simply keep a looseleaf notebook with a page for each child on which notations can be made. Occasionally pages are inserted when special checks are to be made. A summary record may be

---

[1] Sample records are collected at the end of the chapter, pp. 153 ff.

kept in the back of the notebook. In this way, information about a whole class can be seen at a glance. One such summary is shown in Sample 6.

Some teachers prefer index cards to notebooks for recording data—a 5″ by 8″ card for each child. One side is used for noting activities, work completed, and so on. The other side might include notes on difficulties, general comments, outcomes of conferences, and so on.

Whatever the form, it is important that the teacher write up things that happen. Care should be taken to include every aspect of the child's development—his powers of concentration, his attitudes toward learning, personal relationships, social adjustment, emotional development, power to handle problems through his own thinking—all are part of the picture. Value judgments and mere casual statements are to be replaced with material to show the full development of the child. Such data serve useful purposes for planning, for conferencing with parents, and even more importantly for the teacher to use as a basis for his work with the child.

CLASS RECORDS

Certain kinds of information useful to teachers, pupils, and parents can be easily obtained by the recording of such data on large wall charts in the classroom. Butcher paper, large sheets of newsprint, and so on appropriately titled serve as the form. Useful ideas include the following:

1. *Our Interests.* The chart may be divided into columns, one for the child to write his name in, the other in which to record an interest. Notations range widely and include such topics as music, butterflies, snakes, space ships, dolls, dinosaurs, marbles, and rocks. Children add to the chart or delete items as interests change. At times special-focus charts may be added, inviting the children to name their favorite T.V. show, color, singer, record, book, person, food, and so on.

2. *Projects Under Way.* This can be an easy way to keep current on what's going on in the class. The chart can have columns for the child's name, title of project, date started, and date finished. It can serve as a historical record of interesting projects pursued and may even be a stimulus for helping some children think of things to do.

3. *Committees at Work.* Frequently there are groups working together to plan an activity, to prepare a report, to investigate a topic, or to carry on an experiment. Committees at work note on the wall chart the information requested: the names of committee members and a description of their project. Dates can be given if deemed necessary.

4. *Things We Need.* With children free to make investigations of interest to them in a workshop atmosphere, the needed supplies, materials, and other resources take on added importance. A simple chart located near the exit door of the classroom can be very useful. Here children record their

needs as they're discovered rather than telling the teacher. The chart might have three columns: Name, What I Need, and a column "I'll Bring" to be used by the person who agrees to get the needed item. Everyone takes responsibility for supplying resources within his capabilities. Because many items needed will be junk materials, children can certainly accept the responsibility to help out. There will be other items, of course, that the teacher will have to locate. Having the chart by the exit door serves as a reminder of what is needed as the children and the teacher leave for home.

5. *Books We've Read.* Maintaining a record of reading going on is especially good public relations as teachers change from the conventional to the open classroom. Because reading seems to be a national "hang-up," it makes sense to have a special chart showing that children do read. There is also great value in terms of alerting the teacher and the pupils to popular titles and even types of preferred reading material. The recording is a simple matter—just the title of the book. Pupils' names are not recorded here as there is no attempt to set off a competition. By the same token, each time a book is read by someone, he records the title—no tally marks, for they do not clearly show the extent of reading. A long list impresses us more than ten or fifteen titles with a bunch of tally marks beside each title.

Children are free to record a book read without approval or permission of the teacher. What we want is an honest record, and we get it by not pressuring children through competition. We show trust by letting the child decide when he is to record. If questions are raised, it's better to talk privately with the child, making sure he understands the requirements but at the same time leaving it up to him to make the final decision. An occasional mistake here and there is certainly not disastrous; and the child is well aware of his honesty or lack of it if the intent of the wall chart is clear.

Such a chart might be hung as a scroll so that it can be unfurled in full on special occasions, making a "carpet runner of reading." This special focus, although in some ways ridiculous, may be a useful gimmick to assure "the unfamiliar" that children, when left to follow interests, will also use books if they're related to what is being studied.

And for some children, reading takes on a different character when they're freed from the monotonous "textbook reading time."

Through class charts everyone in the group can be kept abreast of what's going on and what the class is like. No special recording time is needed. Pupils record throughout the day as appropriate. Occasionally there may be reminders to bring "charts up-to-date." During the planning or evaluation period, special attention may be directed to a particular chart for one reason or another. Sometimes lively discussions occur because of what someone has recorded, or there may be specific questions some child wants answered.

Because the charts include a collection of raw data, they can be used periodically by a child or a small group as a basis for making a graph of the results, thus recording the results in a more condensed and organized form. With the addition of summary statements about the graph, it's easy to see how the class is growing, changing, and moving. As the year progresses the old charts of raw data and periodic graphs can be collected into large class books so that the "class history" is available for reference and at the same time wall space is free for the current charts.

PUPIL RECORDS

Much of the responsibility for record keeping properly belongs to the child. He not only needs ready information as he thinks through plans for learning, but he needs the data to see growth as well as to spot and check difficulties. Keeping records helps to sharpen a child's sense of historical perspective relative to his own learning. Such case histories contribute to the child's understanding of how he learns and provide starting points for tackling new problems.

Data from pupil-kept records are accessible to the teacher and to parents at times for review and discussion. The teacher and the pupil can review and analyze the information at conference times. General directions for future planning can be discussed, based on the data available. Difficulties may be spotted and areas for gathering additional information noted.

Because the pupil has recorded his developmental history, he can be a full partner in these discussions and make better decisions for next steps as the teacher calls attention to this trend, asks about that, or notes areas of little emphasis.

These records are also useful in communication with parents. The pupil can share and discuss the information at home in normal, natural ways without waiting for the more formalized parent-teacher-child conference.

Some records are primarily focused on what the pupil has done or accomplished. It may be a daily record of reading, math, or language (Samples 7, 8, and 9). The child records what he did in simple form, such as stories read or even number of pages read. Included would be reference reading he might have done for a study or project. If the type of reading, the amounts, or the purposes for reading are noted, it helps to get away from the idea that reading is done only from a textbook. By the same token, on the language arts or math record, a recording of activities should include more than the "textbook" work. Work at learning centers, and the use of games, as well as the use of math or language arts in other projects, might be noted. Again the record can be useful to help children realize that the subject is real and vital and not just what is in a book.

A record such as that shown in Sample 10 is useful for keeping track of science experiments. Although this can be an individually kept record, a similar type could be used as a class record. There would be some advantages to having such information plainly visible for all to see. Children frequently get ideas of what to do from observing what others have done.

Records are sometimes used as aids to broaden the base of activities or to help in the correction of a problem: Tim always seems to read the same type of material and always about similar subjects. He pours over the motor car magazines but seldom uses books, newspapers, pamphlets, or reference materials. A record such as that seen in Samples 11, 12, and 13 might be one way to move Tim toward using a variety of materials and reading about other subjects.

Michele needs to develop vocabulary skills, to extend language power as well as to strengthen spelling. A record and worksheet might help. An example would be

●   Find six new words to study.

INFORMAL TEACHING IN THE CLASSROOM

- Write the word in a sentence.

- Look the word up in a dictionary.

- Make a dictionary of your new words.

Perhaps the difficulty is related to understanding what was read or to getting an overall view of what was read. A record form such as that in Sample 14 could be used. Such a record can also help the child to improve oral reporting.

Sometimes children need to have their attention called to a particular area such as math. John, for example, in his daily work has for some time done very little, if anything, toward learning math or using it. In order to review what he has done, how well it's going, and possible difficulties that need attention, John keeps a record of his activities for a week such as that shown in Sample 15. On Friday, the teacher and John go over his record and decide on next steps.

A pupil's records change as original needs take on less importance and as other directions appear. Records kept by an individual pupil should be of value to him. Seldom do all children need to keep the same record. Children should be encouraged to devise new forms and suggest other ways of recording data. The more the learner is involved in this task, the better the chances that the record will have meaning for him.

PROJECT RECORDS AND REPORT FORMS

A simple project proposal record can help the student think through a particular project or study. The daily planning records discussed in Chapter 3 are overviews of directions to be taken. A more careful outline of the special project, research, or experiment can complement such planning. The record forms in Samples 16, 17, and 18 are useful to clarify the specific plan to be carried out. The teacher might ask that a pupil either discuss the completed record prior to starting the work or turn it in for review. The purpose is not to seek approval but rather to alert the teacher to possible needed resources, to provide information about what is "in the works," and to allow the opportunity for suggestions and comments.

Such a record not only helps the student to see what is involved in the project but later provides data for review as to how good the planning was in relation to the project development and completion. This kind of planning and analysis of plans is valuable in learning how to solve problems in rational ways.

Some children, initially, will need shorter term activities and studies. A log of these activities can be kept on a form such as that shown in Sample 19. The child records a descriptive title, the date completed, and some kind of assessment or evaluation comment.

A few children may need very direct guidance at first. A form such as that in Sample 20 helps to set a plan for work that moves toward the idea of projects or studies rather than assignments ·or questions to answer. The teacher, in the comment column, may draw attention to a particular resource, suggest talking with another child, add an idea, or raise a question or two. The pupil and the teacher may fill out the form together or the pupil may do it independently and then bring it to the teacher for comment.

Reporting on topics, studies, or investigations can become extremely dull and monotonous. Consequently, as much effort needs to be exerted here as in the study phase if children's studies are to become useful resources to the class. A few children are expert in devising and presenting reports; others need suggestions and guidance if they are to improve.

A form such as that in Sample 21 can help children think through what a good report might include. It alerts the teacher to possible equipment needs and also calls attention to the fact that in the master resource guide a notation should be made about the report if it is to be made orally. Many reports, however, are displayed or exhibited with the child available only to answer questions at a stated time.

RECORDS AT LATER STAGES

During the transition stage from conventional teaching toward more informal teaching in the open classroom, the emphasis on records as well as the types of records is probably different from the emphasis and types of records to be used at later stages. Early records frequently maintain some emphasis on common school subjects. Pupils are expected to keep tabs on activities in reading, math, science, and so on, separated from general patterns of working. The record form is frequently more structured and precise in terms of what is expected and possible data to record during the changeover phase. It may be enough at this point to begin to get pupils involved in the whole aspect of recording along somewhat familiar lines. Establishing individual responsibility and the notion that pupils are to be involved in self-evaluation based upon recorded data can be a big step.

There is no smooth, gradual flow from one way of working to another. What and how much to record will vary from child to child, from time to time, and from teacher to teacher. Initially much of the what and how of record keeping will be suggested by the teacher. Even at early stages, though, there should be opportunities for the children to make suggestions and to try out their own ideas. The teacher should be sensitive to the children's growth and encourage individuals to develop their own devices for keeping data regarding learning. Some children will move independently rather quickly. Others may continue to use the teacher's suggestions for a long time. Even children who are moving independently may need concrete suggestions from the teacher from time to time. The teacher and the pupil will occasionally want to review the record-keeping system at conference time to see if changes may be useful.

Children's initial ideas of changing records to be kept are frequently still rather structured. This is, of course, all right because even the smallest step toward a greater acceptance of personal responsibility for learning is to be encouraged. Eventually, however, the teacher may wish to encourage more open types of record keeping. The intent is to begin to break down traditional dividing lines between subjects and to view learning as more related to exploring interests, investigating questions, making studies around meaningful topics, and so on. In effect, the teacher wants to establish that school is not a place where you do reading, math, and spelling but a workshop-laboratory where one can explore and investigate widely about the world in which we live. Nevertheless, school is not a place for just aimless wanderings but a place where one exerts self-discipline and engages in purposeful activity related to personal interests. Consequently some form of record keeping is still appropriate even at later stages of open classroom development. Just as the scientist maintains careful records about his work, the learner does too in order to have data for later review, analysis, and interpretation.

It may help to think of the record system in terms of some kind of a basic recording that is more or less ongoing and special records that are instituted for specific purposes and needs. One such basic record is shown in Sample 22. This is a descriptive log of activities, of how the pupil has spent his time, of notations about next steps, of how things worked, and so on. It is a diary or journal of learning development.

For this basic recording it may be better to move away from a record sheet to the use of a blank notebook such as a composition book for every pupil. The pupil records daily his plans for the day, what actually happened, and a general assessment of the developments and plans.

Special records are used as needed and may vary widely from time to time and from pupil to pupil. At times it will be useful to gather specific data in order to clarify a general trend or to alert the pupil to other areas for exploration. For example, after a pupil-teacher conference in which the daily diary has been reviewed and discussed, it appears that Susan has gotten into a rut of doing about the same things, day in and day out. Most of these seem to be of a short-term nature. There's little depth to the activities. To clarify the situation it is decided that Susan will keep a time record for a few days that will be used in a later discussion. A special form such as that in Sample 23 might be devised. Times, selected at random, are either listed or recorded throughout the day with a notation made of what is being done at that time. Such a record, kept for only a few days, has a special purpose. The intent is to take a sampling over several days of how time is spent to see if there is a need to begin more specific planning or to broaden experiences and so on. It is a way of gathering specific data to be used in a future pupil-teacher conference.

Other special records might focus on the extent of reading over a few days or weeks, the topics or research studies explored during a month's period, the kinds of resources used,

INFORMAL TEACHING IN THE CLASSROOM

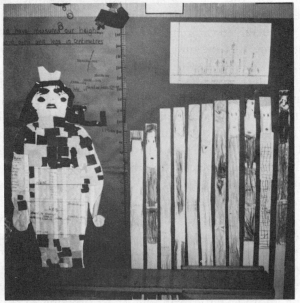

and the work done related to an area such as health or social studies. At times, records such as those discussed in previous sections of this chapter will be modified and used. The development of record keeping is ongoing. With an experimental, research frame of reference, the teacher develops, tests, revises, adds, or deletes, keeping firmly in mind that records are tools, not ends. This development process was described by one teacher as follows:

"RECORD KEEPING–SOME STEPS ALONG THE WAY"[2]

Probably the first record I ever made was a student population study. Using information from the cumulative record I recorded in summary form pertinent data for each student: Name, age, ability level, reading vocabulary and comprehension scores, arithmetic reasoning and fundamental scores, language scores, and health factors. It became obvious that learning situations oriented primarily toward the group could not possible provide for the needs of the class.

The first step I took was to open up in the area of reading. I first developed and used records which would be of help to me as I held individual reading conferences. In a notebook I tried to keep track of the individual reading needs of each child. Then I developed a form which listed specific reading skills. I would mark on this form as I listened and talked with each child during his reading conference. It was not until a few years later that I realized that the child should have this record. He needs to be aware of his needs. Even more than that, he should have a hand in deciding what his problems (needs) are. Now when I have a reading conference, the student keeps the record. Together we look at the form and decide what needs to be done if the child is to improve his reading ability.

The next step I took was to attempt to develop records which students could keep. These records had to be meaningful to them. They had to be records which would allow the student to see his learning growth.

The student now kept three reading records: A reading list of what he was reading (Sample A), a reading continuum which showed what some of his attitudes toward reading were and what skills he needed to work on in both word attack and comprehension areas (Sample B), and an oral reading self-evaluation check (Sample C).

After observing the students keeping records in reading, I decided to attempt to develop record forms which students could use in other areas. I had noticed that in reading, the students seem to find a certain amount of security and deep satisfaction in knowing they could discover their own needs. They began to be the most important person in the classroom and not the teacher. Their ideas were important and they had an important role in their learning.

I found that the records of the students tell the teachers a lot about the self-image of the student. In the records that I had kept I found that my assessments of student needs were very sophisticated but meaningless to the student. As I began to look at the records of the students I found that his informal assessment was very similar to mine. The only

---

[2] Excerpted from materials prepared by Douglas J. Dale describing his development of records over a period of several years.

SAMPLE A

NAME _____

Complete the list each day. It will be a record of your reading.

TEACHER CHECK	DATE	TIME OR TIMES		BOOK, MAGAZINE, PAPER, ETC.	PAGES YOU STARTED AT AND PAGES YOU STOP ON	
		START	STOP		START	STOP

SAMPLE B

READING CONTINUUM

NAME _____

DATES												
1. I choose a variety of books to read. I do not read only one type of book.												
2. I use my spare time to read because I enjoy it.												
3. I can figure out a word I don't know by seeing how it is used in the whole sentence.												
4. I set my own goals. I raise my reading level by choosing more difficult books which I still can read.												
5. As I read, I think about what the author is trying to say.												
6. I can tell about the way the author wrote the book when I finish.												
7. I can tell you about the story in the book in THREE OR FOUR sentences.												
8. Before I have finished a book, I can predict a possible ending from what has gone on before.												
9. I can think up ways of having interesting book reports.												
10. I enjoy telling others about good books I have read.												
11. I ask others about good books they have read.												
12. I do not choose a book because it looks easy to read.												
13. I keep my book list up to date.												

SAMPLE C

ORAL READING SELF-EVALUATION

NAME _____ DATE _____

Select something to read.
Tape your reading for one or two minutes.
Then listen to your tape.
Complete the following.

After listening to the tape I made I think I need to . . .
(check those things you feel that you need to work on)

_____ Select easier reading materials.

_____ Read more smoothly.

_____ Pause after period.

_____ Pause after commas.

_____ Read slower.

_____ Read with more expression.

_____ Read louder.

What else can you do to improve your reading? _____

_____

_____

_____

_____

_____

_____

_____

_____

_____

_____

Do you think that your reading (oral) has improved since the last recording you made?

YES _____ NO _____

difference was that he could understand it. His informal assessment and record keeping had meaning to him. He could see how he was learning how to learn.

It was probably this single discovery that led me to decide that most of my detailed records were a waste of time because they were of no value to the student. Perhaps they did help me to understand the student, but what good is that if the student cannot find some way to see and understand himself. My records meant nothing to him, but his were of great value to him and to me.

The next forms related to work habits, oral language, written language, spelling, handwriting, physical education, and math. I tried to develop records similar to the reading continuum so that the student could assess his strengths in skills, look at his attitudes, and keep track of what he was doing. At last, I was beginning to have a great feeling that I was getting my feet firmly planted as far as individualized instruction was concerned. Then it happened.

Over the years I had continually been adding record keeping to the student's load of work. In the beginning it was great. But as the student was required to keep more and more records he found that a great deal of his time was used for keeping records. What a mistake. Sure, I now had to keep less records and I could spend more time working as a teacher. But what about the student?

He was the most important person in my classroom. I had to do something. After having placed so much thought and work into the records that I developed I was not sure just what to do.

Then I began to think about what had happened in math. My attempts to develop workable forms had not been too successful so I had given each student a blank workbook (notebook). He was asked to write down math problems he wanted to learn about or math that he could not do.

The student and I would look at his workbook and make decisions about next steps. He could then select from books, files, or materials in the math lab to help him develop his math abilities.

Many of the records I started with are no longer used because I feel I no longer need them or because they have been replaced with more successful means. I moved from keeping most of the records to where students now keep most of them. I feel if any form of record keeping is to be helpful to the student, he must be able to use and see the records himself. If records sit in a file for the most part I think they are completely useless. Students must continually use records so that they can see their progress in learning.

Toward the beginning of my search I felt I was finding the answer—the program that would work. But I know now that there is no one answer, no one program. I only know that as long as I teach I will be experimenting, testing out, and increasing my understanding of how I can be a facilitator, a resource, a guide to children engaged in learning how to learn.

SOME CAUTIONS AND POINTS TO CONSIDER

Record keeping, whether done by the teacher, the pupil, or both, can easily become a burdensome chore. Frequently at beginning stages there is a tendency to keep too many records and to record too much detail. If care is not exercised, the time spent on records exceeds the usefulness involved. At periodic intervals the teacher should survey the record-keeping picture. This should include conversations with children to determine their feelings and viewpoints. Each record kept should be reviewed to see if it is still needed, if it adds significantly to the whole picture, or if another form might be better. Basically every record should contribute in some way to the learning growth of the child. "How does it contribute?" is a good question to ponder as records are reviewed. Such guidelines as these may also help:

- Change records to meet new needs; eliminate records as needs are filled.

- Keep records flexible. Involve the pupil in determining "which" records.

- Different records for different pupils may be more appropriate than the same record for all. *Avoid standardizing.*

- Keep the basic record system simple and limited to one or two forms. Use special records for other needs. Limit special records to one at a time, but change them frequently so that a varied picture and many purposes can be served over a period of time.

- Test the proposed record against such questions as these—
  —Is it easy to manage?
  —Does it provide information quickly and easily?
  —Is it simple to use?
  —Does it have a significant purpose?

Records are valuable tools only if they really do the job that needs doing. Recording data for the sake of amassing information does little except make record keeping a chore. Simple records, few in number and fitted to the learner, are best. The record system is all part of helping pupils move forward in "learning how to learn."

SAMPLE 1

CLASS OBSERVATION GUIDE

WEEK OF _____

PUPILS' NAMES	READING	MATH	SCIENCE
Avery, Lucie			
Bonner, Tim			
Butler, Lucky			
Clarke, Van			
Custer, Stan			

SAMPLE 2

PUPILS' NAMES	DATE	COMMENTS/OBSERVATIONS
Atwell, Jake	9/12	Needs work on comprehension / good science / word practice.
Busler, Char.	9/18	Trouble planning / broaden interests.
Butler, Hank	9/8	Reads at home a lot / did exhibit on "How Seeds Grow."
Condor, Vince	9/20	Brought snake to school / interested in animals / works at math center / avoids reading.

154

SAMPLE 3

ANALYSIS OF ORAL COMMUNICATION SKILLS

NAME _____ DATE _____

OBSERVATION GUIDE	YES	NO
Skills		
Speaks directly to point.		
Speaks easily with assurance.		
Has good posture while speaking.		
Uses good speech rhythm.		
Organizes thoughts and presents them in a logical manner.		
Responds effectively to questions and comments.		
Language use is grammatically correct.		
Characteristics of Voice and Speech		
Good pitch of volume.		
Good speech rate.		
Enunciation good.		
Content Impressions (Applicable to Assigned Presentations)		
Shows evidence of thoughtful preparation.		
Material appears accurate and well balanced.		
Uses supplementary aids effectively (e.g., charts, pictures, graphs, slides)		
Other		

SAMPLE 4

MATH PROGRESS

PUPILS' NAMES	1-PLACE MULTIPLIER		2-PLACE MULTIPLIER
	NO REGROUP	REGROUP	
Allan, Sue			
Arval, Henry			
Bane, Joe			
Brush, Marc			

SAMPLE 5

ANALYSIS OF ORAL READING HABITS

PUPIL'S NAME _____

DATES OBSERVED:						
1. Points with finger.						
2. Loses place often.						
3. Repeats often.						
4. Adds words.						
5. Skips words.						
6. Ignores punctuation.						
7. Reads in monotone.						
8. Phrases incorrectly.						
9. Enunciates poorly.						

GENERAL COMMENTS: _____

_____

_____

_____

_____

_____

_____

_____

_____

_____

_____

_____

_____

_____

_____

_____

_____

_____

_____

SAMPLE 6

SUMMARY

DATE	PUPIL'S NAME	TOPIC/PROJECT	PROGRESS	SHARING	DATE FINISHED

SAMPLE 7

MY DAILY READING RECORD

NAME _____

DATE	WHAT I'M READING	NO. OF PAGES	COMMENTS

SAMPLE 8

NAME _____

DATE	WORK ACCOMPLISHED

SAMPLE 9

WHAT I HAVE DONE IN LANGUAGE ARTS

NAME _____ WEEK OF _____

MONDAY: _____
_____
_____
_____
_____
_____

TUESDAY: _____
_____
_____
_____
_____
_____

WEDNESDAY: _____
_____
_____
_____
_____
_____

THURSDAY: _____
_____
_____
_____
_____
_____

FRIDAY: _____
_____
_____
_____
_____
_____

SAMPLE 10

SCIENCE EXPERIMENTS AND INVESTIGATIONS

NAME _____

EXPERIMENT OR TOPIC	DATE STARTED	DATE COMPLETED	RESULTS

SAMPLE 11

READING RECORD

NAME _____

	DATE	BOOK	NEWSPAPER	MAGAZINE	PAMPHLET
Cars					
Animals					
Space Travel					
Sports					
People					
Music					
T.V. Shows					
Movies					
Mystery-Detective					
Insects					
Travel-Adventure					

SAMPLE 12

READING RECORD

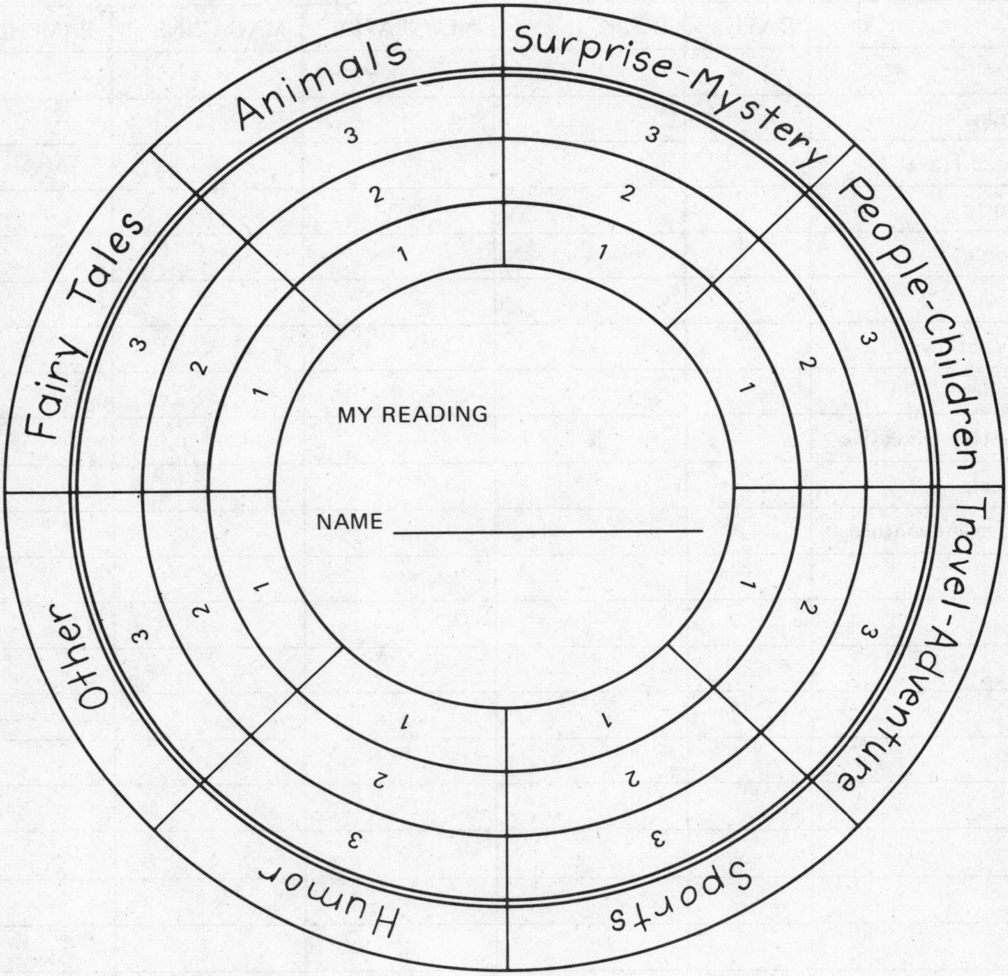
Animals
Surprise-Mystery
People-Children
Travel-Adventure
Sports
Humor
Other
Fairy Tales
3
2
1
MY READING
NAME ___

Color in a numbered space on the wheel under the heading that best describes what you have finished reading.

SAMPLE 13

READING RECORD

NAME _____

	BEGINNING DATE	COMPLETION DATE	AUTHOR—TITLE
Mystery/Detective			
Foreign Lands			
Science-Fiction			
Historical			
Western			
Biography			

SAMPLE 14

READING—WHAT IT WAS ABOUT

NAME _____ DATE _____

BOOK _____

STORY _____

Answer as many questions as you can.

1. What is the story about?
   (Pirates, travel, other children, animals, etc?) _____

_____

_____

2. Name one person in the story. _____

3. Tell one thing that happened. _____

_____

_____

4. Make up another title for the story. _____

_____

5. Write several T-F sentences about your reading. _____

_____

_____

_____

_____

_____

_____

_____

_____

_____

_____

_____

_____

_____

_____

_____

166

SAMPLE 15

WHAT I HAVE DONE IN MATH

NAME _____   _____

MONDAY _Worked at measurement area._
_____Used click-wheel to measure size
of school yard. Also measured room size._

TUESDAY _Began book on shapes._
_____Made patterns._

WEDNESDAY Worked more on shape book.
_____Tried to figure out how to make
a scale from picture in book._

THURSDAY _____

FRIDAY _____

SAMPLE 16

PROJECT PLAN

NAME _____ DATE _____

Topic I'm researching: _____

_____

Questions I'm finding answers to: _____

_____

_____

_____

_____

_____

_____

_____

_____

_____

_____

_____

_____

_____

_____

_____

_____

_____

_____

_____

_____

_____

_____

_____

_____

_____

_____

SAMPLE 17

NAME _____

SUBJECT AREA _____

DESCRIPTION OF PROJECT _____

_____

_____

_____

_____

_____

_____

_____

_____

_____

_____

_____

_____

_____

_____

_____

_____

_____

_____

_____

_____

_____

_____

_____

_____

_____

DATE BEGUN _____

DATE I PLAN TO BE FINISHED _____

SAMPLE 18

PROJECT PLAN

NAME _____ DATE STARTED _____

PROBLEM: Topic or area to be investigated: _____

_____

_____

PROCEDURE: How I plan to go about it: _____

_____

_____

_____

_____

Some things (questions) I want to find out: _____

_____

_____

_____

_____

_____

RESOURCES: Materials I will need: _____

_____

_____

_____

RESULTS: What happened: _____

_____

_____

_____

Teacher comments: _____

_____

_____

SAMPLE 19

SHORT-TERM PROJECTS/ACTIVITY/STUDY

NAME _____

ACTIVITY/STUDY/PROJECT	DATE COMPLETED	RESULTS/COMMENTS
1.		
2.		
3.		
4.		
5.		
6.		
7.		
8.		
9.		
10.		

SAMPLE 20

NAME _____ DATE _____

Write down the topic or study you are doing in each subject area below. This must be shown to me before you start. Also, the completed work must be shown to me.

PLANS	TEACHER'S COMMENTS
Social studies	
Science	
Reading	
Math	
Language	

EVALUATION	YES	NO
1. I worked in a way that did not disturb others.		
2. I returned all of the books and supplies that I used to the right place.		
3. I feel I really accomplished some work today.		
4. Other:		

_____

_____

_____

SAMPLE 21

NAME _____ DATE _____

My report is about _____

_____

_____

_____

I used these materials in my study: _____

_____

_____

_____

_____

My report will include: charts _____ slides _____

                           pictures _____ films _____

                           questions _____ display _____

                           other _____

I would like to give my report on (date) _____

My report should take about _____ minutes.

I will need the following equipment, materials, help: _____

_____

_____

_____

_____

_____

_____

TEACHER'S COMMENTS ON PROPOSED PROJECT REPORT

_____

_____

_____

_____

SAMPLE 22

MY DIARY

NAME _____

Monday, Oct. 5
_____

_____

_____

_____

_____

_____

Tuesday, Oct. 6
_____

_____

_____

_____

_____

Wednesday, Oct. 7
_____

_____

_____

_____

_____

Monday, November 8
_____

_____

_____

_____

_____

_____

SAMPLE 23

TIME AND ACTIVITY RECORD

NAME _____

CHECK POINTS	DATE	DATE	DATE	DATE	DATE
9:00					
9:15					
10:00					
10:45					
11:00					
11:30					
12:00					
12:30					
1:00					
1:15					
2:00					
2:45					
3:00					

At the time listed, record in a word or two what you are doing, e.g., reading, talking, at science area, working on _____ study.

CHAPTER 6

Beginning Steps—
Moving Toward the Open Classroom

First steps are never easy. There are many factors to consider. Ideas revolving around initial thinking tend to be unorganized. Somehow there needs to be a putting together and a plan of action developed.

How to start is unique and different for each individual. The conditions are different. The group of children involved have unique characteristics. Individual strengths of teachers vary. But the experiences and ideas of others can help.

The open classroom involves changing nearly all the facets. To plunge can be disastrous although some teachers have done it successfully. To take some steps may never lead beyond some simple alterations—certainly the open classroom is not achieved overnight. A big mistake so frequently made is to label beginning steps as end results. Problems encountered are misconstrued. They are associated with the goal or focus rather than the process of getting there. Consequently teachers as well as parents may say "It didn't work," "I didn't like it," or "It's no good" without understanding that the implementation or progress made was faulty, not the idea.

Beginning steps are just that. There can be problems that need to be solved. There can be understandings that need to be developed. There can be behaviors, attitudes, and even basic beliefs that must undergo thorough examination and change. This is part of the process of change. Moving toward the fully functioning open classroom that is consistent with the theoretical framework, important assumptions, and application of practices takes time, experimentation, and thought.

Beginnings frequently are not smooth. The transition from a classroom functioning largely under teacher control and direction to a classroom functioning under pupil responsibility and self-discipline can hit highs and lows. The evolving of individual pupil structure to replace teacher structure is not even welcomed by some children. This resistance, along with the many questions that arise, can engender and increase doubts and insecure feelings on the part of the teacher. Knowing about and anticipating such times the teacher prepares in advance and builds confidence by giving careful thought to plans. Some thinking focuses on how individual pupils may respond. The pros and cons of various actions are weighed and possible results anticipated. Recognizing possible pitfalls and children's possible reactions helps to allay anxiety when and if the happening actually occurs. Even the unexpected is not so jolting if the teacher realizes that transitional phases may bring ups and downs.

Keeping notes on developments can be useful. Such records can help the teacher make a more accurate analysis and assessment of progress. Without such notes too frequently only the frustrations are remembered. Certainly valuable clues can be gained from the successes. Patterns may begin to emerge that the teacher can use in planning changes or in developing new facets of the program. Some teachers have kept logs of their development that are used not only for analysis but to help them maintain rigor and consistency in their moves toward a more open program. One teacher's log over a period of several months is included here as an example of what can happen and how things begin to work out.

BEGINNING STEPS MOVING TOWARD THE OPEN CLASSROOM

A TEACHER'S DIARY*

2/13/72

    This log is intended to help me in planning and developing an open or individualized form of education for the children in room 6. Such an effort involves a change in personality on my part and therefore many of my personal and private thoughts and activities past, present, and future may appear in the following pages. Therefore any person other than myself agrees that my private and personal thoughts and events be held in confidence. . . .

    To date I have done a good deal of reading and have attended many classes sponsored by I.C.E.D.** on open education. I have talked with many teachers and other people regarding open education.

    I have attempted many suggested activities in the classroom dealing with open education and I have done a fair job of setting the environment in the classroom.

    I have involved the parents in the classroom. About eight parents come for one hour a week to work in the room with the children or prepare materials for them. Two mothers teach enbroidery twice a week. One mother is starting a baking class on Wednesday morning.

    Environment includes

1. A comfortable, well-stocked library.
2. A writing area where children make books, write and illustrate stories. Different color markers, pencils, pens, crayons, and papers are in this area.
3. Spanish corner with books and rhymes.
4. Word games area.
5. Sound games area.
6. Listening areas (only one record).
7. Baking area (with oven)—to date seldom used owing to teacher's being unable to supervise.
8. Math area—games, balance, books with blank pages for each child, scales (bathroom and table), rulers and sticks, things to count and sort, money.
9. Science—animals—fish, turtles, rabbit, newly hatched chicks from incubator. Children have brought puppies, hamsters, mice, and birds.
    Have attempted SCIS (Science Curriculum Instructional Study) material objects but not yet an activity (have science books—blank papers).
10. Art—painting easel and group painting on larger sheets in hall. Junk art from junk area.

---

    *The author is deeply grateful to the teacher who kept this log of the events, discouragements, and happenings during the process of changing to an open classroom. The teacher was involved in studies conducted by the author and others focused on what the open classroom is like and how it works. The teacher gave permission to use this excerpt with the understanding that it was to be kept anonyomous.

    **International Center for Educational Development

11. Junk area—just beginning.
12. Bulletin boards are owned by children and work hangs from ceiling on twine and fish line—some work is even put on ceiling.
13. Immediate future:
    a. Post office.
    b. Water and sand area.
    c. Construction.
    d. Maybe a store.

This environment should be suitable for the successful conduct of an open structure program. But to date I have been very dissatisfied with both my conduct and the conduct of the children. The children have not accepted responsibility for their freedom—for example *the chicks*. The children just want to hold them and watch them—lie with them. This is all well and good. Some of the children did sketch them, some did write about them. But for the most part they were content to sit and be amused by the chicks. I have been unable to successfully intervene. I know that I have appeared tense and anxious when dealing with the children. Also, to date I have had to leave what I was doing to correct a situation that I considered to be an irresponsible action on the part of one of the students. Upon returning to the individual or group I know I was more tense, upset, irritable and unable to give my full concentration to the child with whom I was working, which, I imagine, blew the lesson or object I had in mind for them.

Tomorrow I begin once more. I have rearranged furniture and I am sending home a note to have all children come from 9-2 instead of half from 8:50 to 9:50, all from 9:50-2:00 and half from 2-3:00.

I am also going to try having children keep a log of activities which I will help them write. For example: a child finishes work in the math area—would write in his log book . . . "I worked on the balance today." At first I will have to help most of the children but this offers a good way for me to call to his attention an evaluation of his activities and his responsibility for them. Should offer time for individual conference. I don't know about this procedure—I may spend all day doing this—would it be a good use of my time . . . the child's time?????

Oh, for those who can't write I would write it in their log and they would copy it after talk.

2/16/72

This is my crying page. I am unable to move activity of most children into any form of depth or deep learning. All their activities seem to stay right on the surface.

Some children did a play today—Little Red Riding Hood. The main show was the chopping down of the trees (children), the play or story line was acted out inside construction paper house—no one could see or hear it. Point is that I couldn't even make that point clear to the children.

I am tired—confused—and truthfully feeling quite sorry for myself and very ineffective in everything I do. If there is anything good happening in the room I can't recognize it. I have spent my total self in the effort to open the classroom and I am seeing little if any good come of it . . . this is both discouraging and defeating. So I feel it is time to drop any thought of class and leave the city for a few days. Hope to start fresh sometime next week.

2/22/72

Hi again. Had a great time over the weekend.

Let's take a look at the children in the room this past morning. Three girls were playing with Playdough which another girl made and brought in, four boys were playing a number and reading game (Sorry), two girls were watching the chicks or turtles or rabbit, one boy was drawing, three girls and one boy were embroidering with two mothers, and four boys were making a trap to catch a possible thief in our post office.

Teacher was walking, asking, talking to the children. At the time I was anxious. Where, oh where, is the depth? Most of these activities are or seem to be surface and very playful.

Where, oh where, is the reading and writing and math and all the other traditional hang-up type activities?

Let's look at the afternoon—not all of it—just a part: *C. = Children:*

    2 C. reading in library
    3 C. looking at animals
    2 C. math game
    4 C. reading and math game (Sorry)
    6 C. writing books about story I read class (this activity was instituted by the C.)

Teacher was more at ease—kind of surprised to see some form of academics.

New hang-up—Did the C. benefit more from the morning activities or afternoon activities?

Had a talk with instructor after Piaget class. Talk centered around activities just written about. I felt better about the C. after talking with him. I don't know why I feel better. Maybe I need a person who knows about this form of education to reassure my efforts.

Saturday Night—2-26-72

WOW! The things that have happened in the last few days—both with the children and with members of the faculty have been unbelievably exciting. First the children. Most of them have displayed responsibility for themselves. They are beginning to think for themselves and ask questions based on their curiosity and move toward investigation. For example, one girl brought some soap to school. She asked what it was made of. I asked her if she would like to make some—*Yes.* Then do you think anyone else would be interested in working with you? She asked around and got 4 other C. who were interested. I told the C. that I didn't know how to make soap and that we might have to find other people or things to help us. We are looking for something to answer our questions.

INFORMAL TEACHING IN THE OPEN CLASSROOM

The children are beginning to verbalize their learning and their activities. I have required that they write what they do in the room in composition books at the end of each day. In two weeks the attitude and awareness of most children concerning their activities and learnings from their activities has been markedly improved. They are beginning to tell each other what they did and learned and what they are going to do next.

The room when the C. are there looks like it is turned upside down and shaken for good measure. The activity is intense. At times I feel like jumping up and down and clapping and yelling with excitement. Five children from upper grades are coming at their lunch recess. They are beginning projects with the C. in the class. One girl is going to study butterflies, how they develop. Two girls from our room are going to bring the cocoons and the upper grader is going to bring the vegetables.

Mrs. H., the half-time aide is interested in clay so she is to find children and people to help her with clay (which I know nothing about).

That ends my writing for now—but hopefully will serve as a record of how it all got started.

3/2

So much has happened. I am very confused again. Children seem to be going downhill. The substitute had a rough time with the children yesterday. It seems children weren't thinking of constructive things to do. Today I read with many of the children—seems like regression is setting in. I think I'm going to set aside 20 minutes a day for quiet reading.

Children didn't seem with it today—sluggish—heads weren't in the right place.

Somehow there just isn't enough reading and writing to suit me. Oh—Oh———caught myself—I must look for positive things tomorrow. If I keep going on the negative I will psych myself out!

Hope I can sleep tonight. 2:00 A.M.—NO SLEEP YET—THIS IS GETTING TO BE A VERY UNHEALTHY HABIT. One of these days I am going to be officially declared crazy—I'm so upset—I can't think straight—confused. Either I am so excited that I can't sleep or so depressed that I worry all night. Why this preoccupation with children? Why can't I have a normal work-a-day routine?

I just broke my pen—put a hole in my door with my fist. Really settled all my problems!

3/3/ Friday

First morning at 7:00 o'clock I found out that I was not the only one who was worried. The first- and second-grade reading specialists arrived at 6:45 Friday morning. These two people have been very opposed to open structure.

At 6:45 I posted the orange open education workshop bulletin in the primary lounge. At 7:00 o'clock I returned to the lounge to meet the two ladies. The conversation went like this: "Good morning, ladies. Oh, where did that bright orange bulletin go? Have you seen it, ladies?" "What bulletin, what was it about?" "I just can't understand it—I just put it there no more than 10 minutes ago. Are you sure you haven't seen it?" "No, you should bring more and set them on the table so everyone can see them." "It's a good thing I just happen to have one more. Could you tell me where I should put it?"

I don't know what happened to the other poster—it doesn't take too much imagination to figure out what happened to it.

This incident did not make me sad because I hope the three of us can now carry on a more open and honest relationship.

Sunday 3/5

I've been working with I.C.E.D. since November trying to learn how to individualize or personalize education with the children in my class and I believe that since November we have been moving toward a form of open education in the classroom. This *moving toward* is both frustrating and rewarding. The closer we get the more I realize that we have much farther to go.

3/7

I read *Exploring Open Structure** last night. I was interested in Dr. Howes' statement on page 47 concerning literacy skills. "I don't know that that's (literacy skills) the real strength in open-structure environment. I'm really not sure that open-structure learning is the strongest way of building literacy skills."

Combine this with Weber's** thought that "True Individualization makes it possible for the child to recognize and express his own purposes, interests, and individual pattern of learning."

These two statements or thoughts have made me *and are* making me realize that open education is not skill-centered but child-centered. Most of my hang-ups in the past have been over skill-centered matters. I realize that I must now try to shift my emphasis to the child and damn the skills for the time being. I must talk to each child about his concerns and interests and at the same time share *both* my concerns and interests. I am going to ask broad questions like those Tyler poses on 37 of *Exploring Open Structure* to get each child to describe surrounding conditions, recall similar conditions and situations, and make judgment on what present and past situations signify. In this way I hope the children under my care can truthfully *recognize* and *express* their own purposes, interests, and patterns of learning.

Let's see what happens.

_____

*Virgil M. Howes, Helen F. Darrow, Robert E. Kenscher, and Louise L. Tyler, *Exploring Open Structure*, 1968 (out of print).

**Lillian Weber, *The English Infant School and Informal Education* (Englewood Cliffs, N. J.: Prentice-Hall, Inc., 1971).

INFORMAL TEACHING IN THE OPEN CLASSROOM

3/9/72

Some good things are going on in the room. There is a good deal of talking which is good—however it is more social talking than project or class-oriented talking. At this point I am very frustrated. I feel like a Christian who professes the faith, goes to church on Sundays and even weekdays, knows the faith but for some reason can't live to the ideals of the faith.

I think I know what is missing in the room, I think I know what I need, but I just can't seem to get it. I need more graphic explanations of possible things to do in the areas. For example, in the junk area all there is is junk; there should be things or pictures of things that could be made from the junk.

The book club is going very well with the girls in it. They are much more interested in their reading and they are beginning to realize that they can help each other to become better readers. The boys in the club are beginning to catch on. The library club is getting off the ground. I think I'll start doing a magic circle thing in sharing the library books they read. We will start to talk about our library books—seven people in this club.

The water area was started this week—it is very wet—also very popular.

4/3/72

This was the first day back after Easter. The children worked very well today. The children showed a real enthusiasm for writing today. Some were recording in their math and science books. Two boys are going to study ocean animals—library books and drawing and writing.

Five children want to plant seeds—they prepared the pots which were found in junk area (plastic bottles). A third-grade boy from Mary's class taught four children how to weave. One boy made a twirly bird from directions found in a book in the junk area. Rosie brought some pictures of a picnic—she wants to make an album using them. Five girls are interested in learning handwriting. Almost all the children want to make *me books* (books about themselves—weight, height, teeth, color of eyes, type of hair, etc.). One boy wants a book about dinosaurs—study may result.

Mrs. S., reading teacher, is working on a play which eight children wrote. So it looks like the class is off to a good start—I only hope I can keep the fire going by putting enough wood on it.

A fourth-grade teacher, who is very open and very exciting, and I have been working, talking, and reaching together for the past month or two. This has been one big help to me and the children.

4/6/72

It really went great today. Most of the children seemed to be deeply involved in what they were doing. Four girls who made stick puppets yesterday were writing and rehearsing a play today. Three boys were making castles. Three girls were reading directions and following them to make phones and lamps in the junk area. Six children were recording what they had done for their incubator yesterday and today. Two boys started a study on whales. Three children were very involved in a Spanish game. Today was a day when some children actually used reading, writing, and math in their studies. I noticed that some children who hadn't read well in the past were outdoing themselves. *It was like magic!*

NAGGING CONCERNS AND QUESTIONS

Questions, questions, questions are seemingly endless as teachers think about changing over or developing the open classroom. With a firm conviction that the direction is right, with an understanding of what open education is and what the basic tenets are, and with a desire to start, the teacher frequently is nagged by the "what if" and "what about" questions. Some of these are hypothetical and may never arise. Others are anticipatory, focused on things that do arise but usually at later stages. With questions whirling through the thinking being done, the teacher may find it a good idea actually to write down the many questions. Making a list, even if answers are not readily available, so frequently helps to alleviate some of the anxiety. And even if the answer is not thought through in advance and the problem should arise, the teacher is not quite as unprepared as he may have been if the problem hadn't even been considered. But, of course, the listing of questions does begin to give the teacher a framework to start on a logical plan to seek solutions, to assess degree of importance, and to think rationally about forthcoming moves.

Some of the common concerns that teachers express during the starting period are discussed here. Many questions could be included but these few with the discussion that follows may help the teacher get started on his own list.

What if the child chooses to do nothing? How do you get students to use their time wisely and responsibly?

We all need what appears to be on the surface idle moments. This can be a productive time in that it frees us to regroup thoughts, establish new directions, gain momentum for the next tasks. Children who choose to do nothing and are not interfering with others may be engaged in thinking processes far more valuable than if they were actively involved in physical ways. The teacher must not be too prone to label inactive behavior as "doing nothing." (Obviously we're assuming that the teacher is aware of physical problems, if any.)

Using time wisely is as much of a learning process as learning to read. Some adults have never learned it well. Yet how we spend time is crucial to our living—enjoyment, solving problems, producing a thing, earning a living, and so on. For children, planning and assessing the effectiveness of those plans in relation to the goal or outcome can provide useful experiences for growth. As pupils are engaged in meaningful decisions, responsibility grows. The more a pupil feels control and power over himself and his learning behavior, the more likely is he to accept responsibility and make a commitment to the decision he has made.

The teacher's role can be crucial. Monitoring rather than policing is far more useful if the child involved in the decision function makes a plan. The teacher monitors—is the behavior consistent with the plan? Is the child working on the plan, and if not is the plan or the momentary activity to be changed? The teacher serves to keep at a conscious level what the child is doing and how it relates to the plan he developed. The intent is not to close down nor prohibit but to help the child maintain a focus on the decisions he has made or may need to alter.

How does the teacher find time to work with individual children in the seemingly in-depth way that is needed in the open classroom?

The teacher must look at how time is spent to find time. In conventional practice the teacher spends time in group teaching, assignment making and marking, directing and overseeing all activity. In the open classroom the teacher's role changes so that children's involvement in learning does not depend on the teacher's direction. The teacher's time is largely spent with individual children and small groups throughout the day. The teacher's work is individual conferencing, talking with children, and interacting in personal ways rather than "teaching."

BEGINNING STEPS MOVING TOWARD THE OPEN CLASSROOM

Are children in an open classroom required to finish a task they begin?

Ask yourself, "Do I always finish what I start?" How many times have you begun reading a book only to find it wasn't what you expected and so you stopped? Perhaps you've left a movie because it wasn't interesting. Maybe an interruption turned you away and when you were free again you started something new. In the process of doing one thing, a discovery or a new path emerged that you decided to follow because the possibility, the opportunity presented, seemed more worthwhile. A part of independent, responsible acting is to know when to stop as well as to know when to continue. To finish something for the sake of finishing is neither virtuous nor productive in terms of spending time wisely. The concern then is not finishing a task per se but rather helping the child think through the task, what it's yielding in terms of usefulness and enjoyment, and whether it's worth continuing. Once a child has gone through the exploring stage and settled on a task or kind of involvement, giving it up is indeed possible. But there is thought involved before taking that action, as there was in making the plan to do it at the start.

What about pupils who never seem to go near the math area or writing or reading? When do you say, "Now you must do so and so"?

Behind these questions is the whole concern that teachers have about the quality of choices pupils sometimes make and whether or not children can be trusted. Implicit is the lingering belief that specialists, curriculum writers, publishers, and teachers really know what is best for children to learn. To take such a position also means that the adult knows what the future will be and has the insight and knowledge to be able to peg the child in terms of his role and participation in the future. The rapidly changing world of today defies such an assumption. The continuing growth of knowledge and the increasing complexity of our world means that each of us can know only the smallest of parts. Diversity among us will help to enrich our living, and schooling should expand, not restrict, our differences.

But there are other points to be considered as we look at

choices children make. Choosing and deciding well is not automatic. We learn from experience and from assessing and evaluating our decisions. What should have been considered? What are the most important factors? What were the best parts of the decision? What went right or wrong? What would I do differently next time? Consideration of these and other questions can help the pupil grow in his power to make good choices.

The teacher is, of course, faced with doubts when pupils seemingly ignore what has commonly been thought important. The action taken really depends on the strength of the teacher, the firmness of his belief that children want to learn and will seek meaningful experiences. The child's curiosity, his love for learning, the growth in power to manage his learning well, and the development of positive feelings about himself as a learner and problem solver are all endangered if he feels that school is largely a place where one does "what the teacher tells you to do."

At a time such as that described by the question it's well to remember that the environment is a powerful factor. How is it constructed in relation to the problem expressed? The teacher is there not to dictate but to assist, to talk with the child about his work, and to facilitate learning. Coverage is not learning and the child, in the final analysis, does pick and choose regardless of our insistence or what we may toss his way.

How do I account to next year's teachers for the things my pupils "were supposed to have learned"?

Teaching is or should be related to children's growth and development. To build a child's education on the expectation of the next year's teacher, the next grade, or another school is to place greater importance on that than on the child. The next year's teacher, just as you did, must start with the child—his interests, needs, and growth. The teacher who is more interested in a curriculum or grade level not only restricts learning to whatever he decides to offer but builds attitudes among children that school is not a place for personal living, growing, and learning. "Turned-off" youth, dropouts, and charges of irrelevance are only a few of the evident outcomes of such a school. What happens to the individual in terms of how he sees himself and how he learns how to learn are even more important considerations.

How do children having experience in this type of activity fit into a traditional setup? How will children leaving the open classroom readjust to a traditional classroom?

Self-discipline, responsibility for actions, ability to make effective learning plans, enthusiasm for learning, and growth in problem-solving abilities are pluses that even teachers in traditional setups acknowledge and welcome. Beginning changes in the traditional setup may even take place as children and their parents begin to demand something better.

Are we doing children a disservice if we always let them do what they want? The world is not that way.

The open classroom not only takes a realistic view but operates on the sound premise that a child's interest in an experience not only facilitates learning progesss but deepens the meaning as well. Making something unenjoyable or forcing children to engage in tasks that are unpleasant certainly does not build positive attitudes or increase the desire to find out. However, the open classroom does not operate on the laissez faire attitude of random behavior. There is a focus: setting goals, planning, carrying out plans, and assessing developments. But the learner actively participates in determining these functions rather than being a passive recipient of teacher direction. Because self-direction and individual responsibility are goals, the teacher functions in ways to help the child in his growth. Such functioning includes active interaction with the learner as he develops and analyzes experiences to clarify meanings and bring to the conscious level understandings, insights, and personal social values. The child's day is an enjoyable experience designed to build rational thinking and problem solving. And this does help prepare the child to function in the world of today as well as in the future.

How can the teacher plan and organize when much of the learning is spontaneous?

INFORMAL TEACHING IN THE OPEN CLASSROOM

Teacher planning takes on different characteristics in the open classroom. In conventional practice, planning is largely related to group teaching and the systematic coverage of material sequentially organized in some fashion. But planning in the open classroom is focused first of all on the individual child. What resources are needed by the child as he continues his chosen project, inquiry, or study? What resources may be useful to help extend interests? How can the environment be changed to support better the pursuits of the children? These and other questions relate to environment building, which is a continually changing process. Other planning questions relate to records, group processes, conferencing, teaching helps, and so on. Daily plans grow out of developments in the classroom. Long-range plans are made related to resources and classroom environment that may be useful. Knowing about children in general in terms of interests, growth, and developments, the teacher does have data upon which to build plans. The difference is that the plans are not necessarily usable at the time and may be discarded depending on what is happening among the children. But teachers do think ahead. As projects get under way, the teacher notes possible developments and attempts to make available supportive resources. The use, though, depends on the child.

How does the teacher plan practical learning experiences?

Teachers plan and develop the environment with the specific group of children's interests and needs in mind. But they also plan with the children themselves. Learning experiences develop as the pupil interacts and involves himself with the materials and with the other children and the teacher. Ideas for practical items for a vibrant learning environment come from many sources. Teacher guides, courses of study, texts, happenings of the day, children's interests, questions from children, and on and on provide clues and ideas of what might be useful. A real difference between conventional practice and the open classroom is the involvement of the pupil in the decisions about how he will use his time, what he will do, and what plan to execute. The teacher's initial role in developing practical experiences is largely focused on developing the environment as a learning resource.

BEGINNING STEPS MOVING TOWARD THE OPEN CLASSROOM

How can parents be used in an open classroom? What types of activities should they do? How might teacher aides be used in the open classroom?

The parent, the volunteer aide and community citizens can contribute in many useful ways. Some have special interests or hobbies that children enjoy learning about or perhaps even starting on their own. Others may have interesting experiences to relate. Still others have special abilities, such as woodworking, art, sewing, or cooking, that they are willing to teach to children who are interested. The open classroom makes available human resources as well as physical resources.

The parent or the community adult is important whether or not he has a special interest, experience, or hobby to talk about. Children working on a study may want to talk about what they're doing. Another study may require interviews with community people to find out about what one does in certain jobs, about viewpoints and reactions, or "what the good old days were like when you were a child." The adult who listens, who can talk to children, hear a story read, hold a model being built, get a piece of required equipment or material, suggest a possible solution to try, or perform a task that is needed but not within the child's capability makes a useful contribution to children's learning. The chief admonition is "Don't play teacher." Instead, be a warm, supportive adult, available to help the children rather than taking over for them.

A caution for teachers to note is not to assign the volunteer or parent to clerical tasks away from the children. Those jobs are better done by salaried workers. The chief reason is that the parent or volunteer who gets involved in the classroom with the children begins to have a commitment that will ensure his returning again and again. If one is stuck in a room doing just typing or making something, then it's easy to begin the "no show." Additional adults for children to use as resources for personal learning make any classroom richer.

Are basics in open education different from those in traditional education? (How basic is reading, math, pupil choice, commitment, independent thinking?) How can you develop the basic reading skills and vocabulary that it is important for the children to have?

INFORMAL TEACHING IN THE OPEN CLASSROOM

The American school has been built on the premise that learning to read, write, and do math were first steps. After these tools were acquired, other learnings could occur. The early years focus on acquiring these tools, and later the child is engaged in the kind of learning that uses these tools. Such schooling is focused more on content, program, and imposed curriculum than on children's interests and actual needs.

The open classroom focuses on children, their learning and growth in thinking and understanding. Learning how to learn is a basic premise around which practices are built rather than an objective to be added after reading, writing, and artihmetic are learned.

A first difference noted between conventional practices and the open classroom is that there is no magical age at which to begin something. The open classroom does have resources related to reading learnings and growth, but at the age of five and a half or six the child is not started in a program of reading. The interest and the need for learning to read unfold gradually as the child, engaged in tasks he has selected, begins to see how the use of books might be helpful and the skill of reading a tool he should begin to acquire. The personal experiences the child has are the starting and the continuing points for the acquisition of the tools he needs, whether they be reading, plotting a graph, writing to record a finding or to tell a story, and so on. Tools are basic to an individual only if the experience he's involved in or chooses to engage in demands their use. In the open classroom, learning the basics is kept in perspective in relation to children's interests, growth in learning, and involvement in expanding experiences. It is recognized that learning is not dependent upon any one tool, whether that tool be reading or using the telephone. But the teacher does provide resources, works to deepen learnings, and adds to opportunities for expanding interests with the understanding that coming to grips with acquiring reading, writing, and math skills can be important assets for the individual.

How the skills are acquired is a second important consideration. Conventional practice stresses the teacher presentation of material in some kind of a sequence outlined not by the learner but by a specialist. The open classroom does not deny direct teaching, but a real difference is that it's a resource to be used by the learner. He's involved in trying to figure out solutions to aid his growth, solutions that include his ideas, teacher ideas, and others. The timing for next steps grows out of personal experiences, not content logic. Sequence is internally ordered by the learner, not externally developed because of content.

Skills could be said to be learned through the "experience approach," which is unique for each learner. It is recognized clearly that of the hundreds of specific identified reading skills, no individual necessarily needs to know all to be an effective reader. In fact, the pattern of specific skills varies tremendously among effective readers. What is true for reading is as true for other skill subjects as well.

In the open classroom the process of a child's thinking is at least as important as, if not more important than, the acquisition of a skill, a knowledge, or an understanding. And along with this the child's attitude toward and his acceptance of the value of something for himself is as important as the acquistion of a thing. What is gained if a child can read but finds it so distasteful that he never does it? How important is a learning if the child is turned off to further learning? What value is a fact or an understanding if the child is without means for future problem solving? How useful is the learning of what is if the child is unable to cope with future change? These and similar questions are thoughtfully considered as foundations for the open classroom functioning fully to be a setting for children as they develop basics.

GETTING STARTED

With first questions and concerns tentatively explored or held in abeyance, the teacher next moves to get something started in the classroom. The environment is probably a first step: What areas will be arranged? What centers can be organized? With ideas firmly in mind, the teacher, over a weekend or a holiday, carries out beginning moves. The classroom takes on a new look and the stage is set.

There is no one way to initiate the program. With the environment set, next considerations focus on getting the children started in the new way of working.

INFORMAL TEACHING IN THE OPEN CLASSROOM

A first stage is introducing the children to the new situation:

- Discuss the way of working—why the change, how it is expected to develop, how problems are to be solved, and so on.

- Show the children around the classroom—point out equipment and materials, describe possible things to do at each area, allow the children to touch and look closely at things, and so on.

- Answer questions, have the children talk about the one thing that interested them most, and so on.

When the children have some idea of what is available and how they're to work, the teacher might ask each child to write on a piece of paper one area he would like to explore further and one thing he might do there. He brings the "plan" to the teacher for comments, suggestions, and approval. (If the area is too crowded because of other children working there, the teacher might help the child make a second choice. Younger children who can't yet write might tell their choice to the teacher after thinking about it at their seats.)

As the children are working, the teacher goes around the room asking questions, making suggestions, or discussing the work underway. The teacher, initially, makes some contact with as many children as possible. The intent at this point is to sustain the flow of work, iron out minor snags quickly, prevent possible mishaps or arguments, and make sure children know how to use the materials. Basically this first engagement is an exploring time, with the children getting familiar with the new environment.

As interests begin to wane or after a reasonable amount of time spent exploring, the teacher calls the group together for a discussion—what did you do? What problems developed? How did you like the period? What else might you do? At this point the idea of cleaning up an area when through may be brought up. Tentative decisions reached about straightening up and leaving the area clear for others may be written on the board or chart as future reminders. Note that this is different than the end-of-the-day cleanup. The focus here is to have the area ready for use by others during the day. If the area is vacant it should not be cluttered and messy for the child who might want to start work there.

Continued explorations similar to what has been described may be further steps. The teacher might even do some assigning at this point in order to broaden the children's explorations and develop as much familiarization as possible. Whether this takes a day or several depends on the time allotted to this way of working and on the children involved. There will be frequent discussions by the class, small groups, and individuals with the teacher to settle organizational and management problems and procedures. But as the children begin to become familiar, the teacher begins to feels comfortable, and some of the kinks are ironed out, it is time to move to the next stage.

The second stage begins to focus on the quality of work being done as well as on the development of the children's planning, recording, and assessing of growth. At first the teacher works quite directly to help children make good choices and enlarge ideas to include more than a quick, simple response. The class planning meeting can focus on having each child write what he intends to do. Some plans can be reviewed orally and teacher suggestions made as to what else might be included. Other children can add to their ideas from this. At this point directions can be given that the plan or the proposed study include some reading, some writing, a picture or model, and so on.

Some children will need more help than others. One way to handle this without delaying all the children is to let those who feel they have good plans begin. The teacher can review next the plans of those children who aren't quite sure if they're ready to start. As each plan is okayed, the child moves out to begin. Gradually the group size becomes smaller and smaller until the teacher can work quite concentratedly with the few who are having difficulty in making plans. For these children the teacher may have to suggest a specific plan or even assign a task.

As the children work the teacher moves around to hold individual conversations, to offer suggestions, to add resources, and so on. At this stage when a child finishes his work he reports to the teacher. The teacher then reviews the study,

INFORMAL TEACHING IN THE OPEN CLASSROOM

perhaps suggesting additional work or asking the child to make a plan for what he intends to do next.

During this stage the general way of working will evolve. Discussion periods are scheduled periodically for children to share results or progress. How to assess planning and evaluate the quality of the work done are also included at these times. Different planning forms may be introduced and tried out and longer-range planning may be begun with a few of the children.

Record keeping and the kinds of records will be another facet to develop. The involvement of children in adding to the environment can begin to be developed. Group work and projects will be started as individual studies and interests show possibilities of being linked to make exhibits, investigations, murals, or whatever it may be.

Much is really developed during this stage. Consequently the time involved can be quite lengthy. Slow and steady progress focused on a facet or two at a time will prevent difficulties later. If the class is used to teacher direction and control then the changeover to accepting individual responsibility and self-direction is gradual. And the evolvement of quality work from the open classroom does not just happen. Positive teacher involvement in the child's work is a major contributing factor to help children in their growth along this dimension.

These stages lay solid foundations for the fully functioning open classroom. However, other steps are needed and a full implementation of Stage Two does not necessarily lead to the eventual goal desired. Consequently the teacher must be consciously aware of developments and question practices. At this point the teacher will want to look at such questions as these:

1. Is the classroom environment constantly evolving and changing according to the children's needs and interests? Are the children significant forces in the development and creation of the environment?
2. Are the children free to pursue activities and studies without reporting to the teacher or receiving teacher input? Are children free to "turn off" the teacher but also free to seek help without the teacher's treating the request as an opportunity to continue on paths of importance to him rather than to the child?

3. Is the functioning of planning, recording, and assessing a chore or a real help to the child? Are changes readily made? Do individual children utilize these management and organizational tools differently?
4. Is the teacher intervention "constructed" to fit the particular need of the child as he sees it or is it a subtle form of manipulation? Is the conversation honest, as between two interested parties, or being used as a directing force? Is the teacher engaged in the learning process or in a teaching process?

Thoughtful consideration of these and other questions can help the teacher to move into Stage Three—the open classroom. What may initially have been techniques or simple practices are now rounded and deepened with understanding. Implementation emerges from knowing the theoretical considerations and underlying assumptions. The "what" and "how to do it" is created rather than copied. And teacher response grows and develops from philosophical and psychological bases to be constructed in the context of the child and the situation.

MAKING THE CHANGEOVER

In the process of thinking about getting started, these two questions seem to occur:

1. Will the changeover be with a whole class, a group, or a few individuals?
2. Is the initial changeover to be for the whole day, part of the day, or at intervals during the week?

Whether the changeover should be made with the whole class or a group depends on the children involved and how comfortable the teacher feels. No one way has proved best. All ways have worked where there was sufficient thinking through steps and planning in advance. Some of the variations tried include the following:

● A few of the most responsible, mature students were

invited to try this new way of working. The teacher introduced and explained the program. Frequent discussions were held with the small group. As the working pattern began to operate smoothly with these children, others were invited to participate. They were teamed up with the first groups, who helped the new ones become accustomed to the change. Gradually the teacher had the entire class working at various stages as he moved to make the change to the open classroom.

- The class was divided into four equal groups on a rather heterogeneous basis. While three groups pursued their usual studies, the teacher worked with the fourth group to introduce them to the new program. On a rotating basis each group would work part of the day in the new program and part of the day in their normal pattern. Gradually the time was lengthened for each group to work in the new program and a merging of groups began—from four to three to two until eventually the whole class was working this way.

- The whole class was introduced to this way of working. The teacher continued the normal studies but the child could choose to work in the new way or to continue in the familiar pattern. There were class meetings along the way to discuss concerns and problems or to clarify procedures. The children who had largely continued the regular pattern were asked to participate in these discussions. As the time progressed, more and more children began to spend more and more of their time in the new way of working until the changeover was largely complete.

No matter which method the teacher decides on, it's helpful to remember that the plan should fit the children involved. To move too fast can make some children feel very insecure, whereas other children are anxious and willing to try anything new. It can be useful to continue the normal pattern at least as a choice. This frees children to move or change at their own rate rather than being forced to abandon old practices for new. And at beginning stages there can arise the necessity to ask one, two, or three children to continue in the old pattern because of the disruptions they create. If their behavior is handicapping the development of a smooth operation, it's better to work out the new program with the other children and get it operating satisfactorily before trying to bring in the particular children who were creating difficulties.

Once the question "Who is to involved?" is decided upon, the question "For what portion of the day?" arises. Again, various patterns have been successfully employed. Sometimes a beginning is made in one designated period a day. The focus is on the children's making choices of what they will do. The teacher, as previously noted, would make suggestions, help the children with tools and equipment, answer questions, and encourage the children at their work. This period is alternated so that the children do not get the idea that it is unimportant or just for play. If the period were always in the afternoon, it could soon get labeled as "something to keep us busy after we've done our work." From the first the period must be felt to be of great importance so that as much value is attached to the new way of working as was attached to the old. Even to start it would be more impressive if the period selected were a prime time, so to speak, than, say, a Friday afternoon.

There is good reason to place the free choice period at the beginning of the day or right after recess or lunch. This enables children to continue activity without having to change their behavior abruptly. "Settling down" takes place more easily if the child can begin something of his choice as he enters the room rather than having to wait for a "class lesson" to start. The first period of the day is an excellent time to begin because, at first, the discussion that follows such a period can be the starting point for reading and writing activities.

Some teachers prefer starting with half a day. Again, care should be exercised to make sure that some of these half days fall in the morning as well as the afternoon. Children should not get the idea that the new way of working is not an integral part of their day.

Other teachers have started by using the whole day with the previous normal practice occasionally inserted. Eventually such periods drop off and the whole day is spent in the open classroom practice. What part of the day to start with again depends upon the children, the situation, and the comfort of the teacher. For some the changeover is more easily made and problems handled better if there are initial time limits. Others prefer a longer time approach as they attempt to get the operation running smoothly. Whatever the initial decision, the teacher should feel free to adjust and change as new conditions arise.

ALONG THE WAY—HANDICAPS FELT AND STRENGTHS DEVELOPED

Each teacher moving toward developing the open class-room has different initial concerns as well as assessments of progress made. Informal teaching is different from conventional teaching and frequently at odds with past experiences of schooling or teacher training. The fact that teachers do change and develop new skills and professional competencies is significant and noteworthy.

The responses teachers have made when asked about the handicaps that prevented them from moving toward open education as fast as possible provide insights into the process of change. The author has asked numerous teachers this question over the years. Deliberately the request has been made that external factors such as large classes or administrative factors not be named. Instead each participant was asked to concentrate on why he was not able to implement as much as he felt he knew about open education. The following responses are typical:

- I don't trust myself yet; I'm afraid I can't see next steps when children are free to decide which studies they are going to pursue.

- I'm still hung up feeling that I must check everything every day.

- I've come a long way but I still rely on just using open times rather than opening up my class entirely.

- I feel at a loss to know how to extend various learnings.

BEGINNING STEPS MOVING TOWARD THE OPEN CLASSROOM

- I'm really afraid that the children aren't going to accomplish everything they should.

- I feel a lack of confidence in being able to make a wise choice or in allowing a child to make a choice. There's the problem of being able to trust a child's judgement. And I also feel handicapped because I don't know how to deal with other staff members who do not approve of my teaching style.

- I feel a strong responsibility that children learn to read. When children choose not to read books I feel I have failed to reach them. Sometimes I can really feel great about what is going on and then at other times I worry about time's being wasted.

- I guess I'm really afraid my children won't learn if I leave it to their own choice.

- I have too great a desire to know where each child is in order to help him take the next steps. I fear that certain children are not getting any place and then I have a frustration of not being able to do in practice what I know in theory.

- I feel a lack of security in most areas of teaching, not just open education. I feel confident in the actual subject matter but not in my ability to teach effectively, whether in open education or not.

- I have some fear of loss of control, that I won't have things well in hand. Also, there is some desire to be the center of attention, to be needed, and depended upon. There is some fear of failure—that I won't be as good at it as I think.

- When things don't seem to be ongoing and children stop their initiated projects I have feelings of failure that handicap how much I'm willing to do.

- I have had a hard time changing my idea that a good

classroom is a quiet one. I also feel that I want to be in control too much of the time but am working at helping them make decisions more often.

- My personal handicap centers on not trusting myself to "let go" of the traditional way I've done things. Intellectually I believe in open education but emotionally I'm held back—distrust of myself and concern about parent criticism.

As teachers begin work to develop the open classroom, some questions subside and others develop. Much reading, even courses, workshops, and seminars are completed as teachers seek new understandings, insights, and practical help. But some gray areas in terms of understanding or implementing the open classroom remain. When such experienced and knowledgeable teachers were asked what questions they still had, responses such as these were typical:

- What should I expect during a day—how many failures and what is a failure?

- How do I use the questioning-inquiry way in working with children without putting my influence on them?

- How open is a truly open classroom and how does one determine whether or not he is successful?

- I'm not sure about how to extend a child's learning. Sometimes I just happen to get an insight into the situation and the possibilities of extending learning. Often, however, I just don't know what steps to take next.

- How do I sustain interest or work for closure rather than allowing just a fade-out of the child's initiated project?

- How do I get the entire class to be productive? How much structure do I bring to the class? I am confused as to the proper interest centers. How much of my own time and money should I put into the classroom?

- I am not sure about extending open education into all areas of the curriculum. Also math skills and other similiar skills are still a gray area to me, but with more work I'm sure I can solve these problems.

- I bog down in the details; for example, allowing a child to work on something he is interested in is no problem, but whether I enter in or not, and how, is not fully understood.

There are gains as teachers begin to work this way. Individual strengths and a feeling of confidence develop. The areas of growth vary from teacher to teacher as one would expect. But based upon their work and study, these experienced teachers responded to the question, "What areas do you feel you have a good understanding of and could implement fully providing the conditions were right?" like this:

- Room environment and meeting children's interpersonal needs.

- Achieving a good mental if not physical learning environment for my students. I have learned to meet each child as an individual.

- Individualized reading—how to use library books and the personal library for reading.

- Organizing the space in my room to provide a variety of working areas and a visually exciting room.

- My relationships with my children in my class and the emotional environments and attitudes that I see developing.

- I'm running a good individualized reading program in which each child is working with interest at his own level.

- I have done a good job in creating enthusiasm for working at a project that a child really enjoys. They work singly or in groups depending on how they feel.

INFORMAL TEACHING IN THE OPEN CLASSROOM

- I'm doing a good job at eliminating as much failure from my classroom as possible. I intend to keep "weeding out" failure.

- I feel I am doing a good job in giving my children a lot of freedom, especially in the area of math.

The comments, questions, and statements recorded here are from the same group of teachers. Although it isn't possible to trace an individual teacher's growth in thinking, one can see the general development of the group—how they looked at handicaps, what questions develop after experience, and what kinds of strengths develop after work and study. For the beginning teacher, checks along the way can help to bring out not only remaining handicaps but the gains made so far. A focus on "my strengths" helps to build needed reinforcement and motivation for what lies ahead. By the same token a look at handicaps that are within "my" power to conquer are much more helpful to note than handicaps over which "I" have no control. That which can be changed by the individual is a starting place. Other factors may take group action that can also occur as individuals gain power by demonstrating solutions to beginning problems. In the classroom the teacher is a key agent. Behind the closed door significant beginnings of the open classroom can flower.

SOME SIGNS OF CHANGE—GUIDEPOSTS

As the open classroom develops there are signs to observe that indicate change. Conventional practices are replaced. The teacher's role has new dimensions. Children are engaged in a different way. The look of schooling takes on a new focus. And the outcomes reflect deeper dimensions. Some signs are subtle; others more visible. As beginning first steps grow and develop, the observer notes such candid shots as these:

- The classroom environment becomes a rich and good place for living and learning.

- The children's learnings stem more from activity and experience than from texts and assignments.

- The work day flows rather than being chopped up into periods.

- Spelling lists, formal exercises, and math drills are rarely used. Formal lessons to the class virtually disappear.

- The book resource environment is focused on all kinds of books and reference materials rather than being dominated by multiple copies of the same book.

- The concern for the individual child is evident and an important focus.

- Evaluation is focused on self-assessment. The teacher's main concern is with what's happening to the child in the process of learning, how he thinks and tackles problems, rather than with the specific knowledge acquired.

- What a child is growing into rather than what he knows is a goal of prime importance.

- Teaching is supporting, facilitating, being a resource to the child as he develops and tries out the system for learning. The child has responsibility for thought and initiative rather than being a passive recipient of assignments.

- School is living, contributes to living, and enriches it rather than being an interruption or a separate program to be covered.

- There is less imposition of the adult on the child. The doing begins with the child—he creates, invents, discovers, tries out, explores, and experiments. His ideas are the starting points for thoughtful action.

- The child knows what he has done, what he's doing, and even what he plans to do.

INFORMAL TEACHING IN THE OPEN CLASSROOM

Signs such as these help to assure the teacher that progress is being made. The teacher does not expect the open classroom to be a panacea. There is no perfect solution. Success is gained slowly and depends on many factors. But for teachers who are strongly committed to the basic tenets of the open classroom and its emphasis on personal learning, democratic behavior development, and "learning how to learn," the opening of doors to get started is a rewarding professional experience. One teacher summed it up this way:

As a beginning teacher, the only thing I knew was what was taught to me by teachers who probably hadn't taught children for years—if at all. The "what" of teaching was all presented in a book written by someone who doesn't teach. There was nothing in my background to help me teach except earlier experiences dealing with children. Though young, my experiences in school consisted of a teacher lecturing to me and doing my assigned page in a book when everyone else did it. To me, that was teaching and that's what I was going to do.

But nothing taught me as much as going into the classroom myself and actually teaching.

My children in the middle-class school where I student-taught did everything just like the book. But my first class as a regular teacher in a lower economic area did not fit the books. Just because one is "supposed" to do such and such does not make it happen.

My experience has taught me that a child who is quiet may not be learning any more than a disruptive one. The child who can recite his multiplication tables may not know when or how to use them in practical situations. One *cannot* force a child to use them or to learn. He may go through the mechanics, but that is all.

I believe it is time that all the books are thrown out and prospective teachers be put right into the situation of teaching. I also feel that those who write the books should go into the classroom themselves to prove to themselves what is going on and how things and times have changed. They should also look at themselves.

What adult searches out things and learns in a confining situation? Who feels like eating the *same* breakfast at the *same* time every day? What adult doesn't gain more when he's enjoying what he's doing and is interested in it? Who likes doing what someone else wants him to do when *they* want him to do it?

Children are the same. I have seen my children read more when they want to than when I told them what to do. My children are more active and interested and happier doing things on their own which are relevant. Because the school-adopted materials mean little or nothing to them.

And if I am any judge, they're learning as much as, if not more than, my first classes.

—Janice Taxon[1]

---

[1] Janice Taxon teaches in the Marvin Avenue School, Los Angeles Unified School District.

Selected References

There is a growing body of literature with particular relevance for the open classroom concept. These listings sample a few of the many available materials. To help the reader extend his thinking and understanding of informal teaching the references are arranged by chapters. Obviously many titles are relevant to more than one chapter, nevertheless a title is placed where it seems to be particularly strong in reference to the chapter content.

DESCRIPTIVE OVERVIEW

Blackie, J. *Inside the Primary School.* London: HMSO, 1967. (In U.S., British Information Services, New York, N.Y. 10022)

Brown, Mary, and Norman Precious. *The Integrated Day in the Primary School.* London: Ward Lock Educational Co., Ltd., 1968. (New York: Agathon Press, Inc., 1970.)

Center for Curriculum Renewal and Educational Development Overseas. *Children at School: Primary Education in Britain Today.* London: Heinemann Educational Books, Ltd., 1969.

Clegg, Sir Alec. *Revolution in the British Primary Schools.* Washington, D.C.: NAESP, 1971.

Featherstone, Joseph. *Schools Where Children Learn.* New York: Liveright Publishing Corp., 1971.

Holt, John. *The Underachieving School.* New York: Pitman Publishing Corp., 1969.

Howson, Geoffrey. *Children at School: Primary Education in Britain Today.* New York: Teacher's College Press, 1969.

I.C.E.D. *Children in the Open Classroom.* Encino, Calif.: International Center for Educational Development (16161 Ventura Boulevard), 1973. (Designed by Darlene Fear.)

Kohl, Herbert R. *The Open Classroom.* New York: A New York Review Book, 1969.

———. *36 Children.* New York: The New American Library, Inc., 1967.

Kozol, Jonathan, and others. *Radical School Reform.* New York: Simon & Schuster, Inc., 1961.

Mason, Stewart C. *In Our Experience.* London: Longman Group Ltd., 1970.

Murrow, Casey, and Liza Murrow. *Children Come First.* New York: American Heritage Press, 1971.

National Elementary Principal. Perspectives on Open Education. Washington, D.C.: NAESP, November 1972.

Nyquist, Ewald B., and Gene R. Hawes, Eds. *Open Education—A Source Book for Parents and Teachers.* New York: Bantam Books, Inc., 1972.

Open Door: Informal Education in Two New York City Public Schools. New York: Center for Urban Education, 1970.

Peaker, G. F. *The Plowden Children 4 Years Later.* London: National Foundation for Educational Research in England and Wales, 1971.

Peters, R. S. *Perspectives on Plowden.* London: Routledge & Kegan Paul, Ltd.; and New York: Humanities Press, 1969.

Plowden, Lady Bridget, and others. *Children and Their Primary Schools: A Report of the Central Advisory Council for Education.* London: Her Majesty's Stationery Office, 1966.

Program Reference Service. Open Door. New York: Center for Urban Education, 1971.

Rathbone, Charles H. *Open Education: The Informal Classroom.* New York: Citation Press, 1971.

Rogers, Vincent R. *Teaching in the British Primary School.* New York: Macmillan Publishing Co., Inc., 1970.

Rotzel, Grace. *The School in Rose Valley.* London: Metheun & Co., Ltd., 1971.

Silberman, Charles E. *Crisis in The Classroom.* New York: Vintage Books, 1970.

———, Ed. *The Open Classroom Reader.* New York: Vintage Books, 1973.

Sutton, Audrey. *Ordered Freedom.* Encino, Calif.: International Center for Educational Development, 1970.

Walters, Elsa H. *Activity and Experience in the Infant School.* London: National Froebel Foundation, 1951.

SELECTED REFERENCES

Weber, Lillian. *The English Infant School and Informal Education.* Englewood Cliffs, N.J.: Prentice-Hall, Inc., 1971.

CHAPTER 1. A FOCUS ON ASSUMPTIONS, RATIONALE, AND GUIDELINES

Association for Supervision and Curriculum Development. *Human Variability and Learning.* Washington, D.C.: ASCD, 1961.
————. *A New Look at Progressive Education,* Washington, D.C.: ASCD, 1972.
Barth, Roland S. *Open Education and the American School.* New York: Agathon Press, Inc., 1972.
Boyle, D. G., *A Student's Guide to Piaget.* Oxford: Pergamon Press, 1969.
Brearley, Molly, and others at the Froebel Institute. *Fundamentals in the First School.* Oxford: Basil Blackwell, 1969.
Brearley, Molly, and Elizabeth Hitchfield. *A Teacher's Guide to Reading Piaget.* London: Routledge & Kegan Paul, Ltd., 1966.
Furth, Hans G. *Piaget for Teachers.* Englewood Cliffs, N.J.: Prentice-Hall, Inc., 1970.
Glasser, William. *The Effect of School Failure on the Life of a Child.* Washington, D.C.: NAESP, 1971.
————. *Schools Without Failure.* New York: Harper and Row, Publishers, Inc., 1969.
Helmore, G. A. *Piaget, A Practical Consideration.* London: Routledge & Kegan Paul, Ltd., 1969.
Holt, John. *Freedom and Beyond.* New York: E. P. Dutton & Co., Inc., 1972.
Illich, Ivan. *Deschooling Society.* New York: Harper and Row, Publishers, Inc., 1970.
Isaacs, Nathan. *Early Scientific Trends in Children.* London: National Froebel Foundation (no date).
Leonard, George B. *Education and Ecstasy.* New York: The Delacorte Press, 1968.
Miller, Susanna. *The Psychology of Play.* London: Penguin Books, Inc., 1968.
National Froebel Foundation. *Some Aspects of Piaget's Work.* London: National Froebel Foundation (no date).
Perrone, Vito. *Open Education: Promise and Problems.* Bloomington, Ind.: Phi Delta Kappa Education Foundation, 1972.
Peters, R. S. *Ethics and Education.* London: George Allen and Unwin, Ltd., 1966.
Piaget, Jean. *The Child's Conception of Time.* London: Routledge & Kegan Paul, Ltd., 1969.

_____. *The Language and Thought of the Child.* London: Routledge & Kegan Paul, Ltd., 1959.

_____. *Science of Education and the Psychology of the Child.* New York: Orion Press, 1970.

_____, and Inhelder, Barbel. *The Psychology of the Child.* London: Routledge & Kegan Paul, Ltd., 1969.

Weinstein, Gerald, and Mario D. Fantini. *Toward Humanistic Education—A Curriculum of Affect.* New York: Praeger Publishers, Inc., 1970.

Yardley, Alice. *Exploration and Language.* London: Evans Brothers, Ltd., 1970. (New York: Citation Press)

_____. *Reaching Out.* London: Evans Brothers, Ltd., 1970. (New York: Citation Press)

Yeomans, Edward. *Education for Initiative and Responsibility.* Boston, Mass.: National Association of Independent Schools (4 Liberty Square), 1968.

CHAPTER 2. A FOCUS ON THE LEARNING ENVIRONMENT AND CURRICULUM

Anastasiou, Clifford J. *Teachers, Children, and Things: Materials-Centered Science.* Toronto, Canada: Holt Rinehart & Winston of Canada, Ltd., 1971.

Arneil, Isobel S. *Infant Handwork* (The Teaching Aid Series 4). London: Thomas Nelson and Sons, Ltd., 1970.

Cohen, Donald. *Inquiry in Mathematics via the Geo-Board.* New York: Walker & Company, 1967.

Darrow, Helen Fisher, and R. Van Allen. *Independent Activities for Creative Learning.* New York: Teacher's College Press, 1961.

Dean, Joan. *Language Areas.* London: Evans Bros., Ltd., 1972.

_____. *A Place to Paint.* London: Evans Bros., Ltd., 1972.

_____. *Working Space.* London: Evans Bros., Ltd., 1972.

Early Childhood Education Study. *Materials: A Useful List of Classroom Items That Can Be Scrounged or Purchased.* Newton, Mass.: Educational Development Center, 1970.

EDC. *Cardboard Carpentry.* Newton, Mass.: Educational Development Center, 1968.

EKNE. *Multi-Age Grouping: Enriching the Learning Environment.* Washington, D.C.: EKNE, 1968.

Friauf, Frances C., and Peggy B. Hobbs. *Games for Learning Mathematics.* Nashville, Tenn.: Project Mid-Tenn Brookmeade Elementary School, 1969.

Holt, John. *What Do I Do Monday?* New York: E. P. Dutton & Co., Inc., 1970.

Holt, Michael. *Science Happenings.* London: Ginn and Company, Ltd., 1969.

Jackson, Brenda B. *Models from Junk.* London: Evans Bros., Ltd., 1971.

Kahl, David H., and Barbara J. Gast. *Learning Centers in the Open Classroom.* Encino, Calif.: International Center for Educational Development, 1974.

King, Pat H. *Games That Teach.* Encino, Calif.: International Center for Educational Development, 1971.

Matthews, Geoffrey. *Mathematics Through School.* London: John Murray, 1972.

Nuffield Foundation. *Mathematics—The Later Primary Years.* New York: John Wiley and Sons, 1972.

Nuffield Mathematics Project. *I Do and I Understand.* New York: John Wiley and Sons, 1967.

Povey, Gail, and Jeanne Fryer. *Personalized Reading.* Encino, Calif.: International Center for Educational Development, 1972.

Schools Council. *The New Curriculum.* London: Her Majesty's Stationery Office, 1967.

Veatch, Jeannette. *How to Teach Reading with Children's Books.* New York: Citation Press, 1968.

Wurman, Richard Saul, Ed. *Yellow Pages of Learning Resources.* Cambridge, Mass.: MIT Press, 1972.

CHAPTER 3. A FOCUS ON ORGANIZATION AND PLANNING

Cook, Ann, and Herb Mack. *The Pupil's Day.* New York: Citation Press, 1971.

Ridgway, Lorna, and Irene Lawton. *Family Grouping in the Primary School.* London: Ward Lock Educational Co., Ltd., 1965. (New York: Ballantine Books, 1973).

Taylor, Joy. *Organizing and Integrating the Infant Day.* London: George Allen and Unwin, Ltd., 1971.

Walton, Jack. *The Integrated Day in Theory and Practice.* London: Ward Lock Educational Co., Ltd., 1971.

CHAPTER 4. A FOCUS ON THE TEACHER'S ROLE

Ashton-Warner, Sylvia. *Teacher.* New York: Simon & Schuster, Inc., 1963.

Brearley, Molly, Ed. *The Teaching of Young Children: Some Applications of Piaget's Learning Theory.* New York: Schocken Books, Inc., 1970.

Bremer, John, and Ann Bremer. *Open Education—A Beginning.* New York: Holt, Rinehart & Winston, Inc., 1972.

Cass, Joan, and D. E. M. Gardner. *The Role of the Teacher in the Infant and Nursery School.* London: Pergamon Press, Inc., 1965.

Darrow, Helen F., and Virgil M. Howes. *Approaches to Individualized Reading.* New York: Appleton-Century-Crofts, Inc., 1960.

Howes, Virgil M. *Individualization of Instruction: A Teaching Strategy.* New York: Macmillan Publishing Co., Inc., 1970.

Marsh, Leonard. *Alongside the Child in the Primary School.* London: A. & C. Black, Ltd., 1970.

Moustakas, Clark. *The Authentic Teacher.* Cambridge, Mass.: Howard A. Doyle Publishing Company, 1967.

Thatcher, David A. *Teaching, Loving, and Self-directed Learning.* Pacific Palisades, Calif.: Goodyear Publishing Co., Inc., 1973.

Veatch, Jeannette. *For the Love of Teaching.* Encino, Calif.: International Center for Educational Development, 1973.

————— and others. *Key Words to Reading: The Language Experience Approach Begins.* Columbus, Ohio: Charles E. Merrill Publishing Co., 1973.

Wolfson, Bernice. *Moving Toward Personalized Learning and Teaching.* Encino, Calif.: International Center for Educational Development, 1969.

Yardley, Alice. *The Teacher of Young Children.* London: Evans Brothers, Ltd., 1970. (New York: Citation Press, 1971.)

Yeomans, Edward. *Preparing Teachers for the Integrated Day.* Boston, Mass.: National Association of Independent Schools, 1972.

CHAPTER 5. A FOCUS ON RECORDS AND EVALUATION

Beegle, Charles W., and Richard M. Brandt, Eds. *Observational Methods in the Classroom.* Washington, D.C.: Association for Supervision and Curriculum Development, 1973.

Chittenden, Edward A., and others. *Analysis of an Approach to Open Education.* Princeton, N.J.: Educational Testing Service, 1970.

Combs, Arthur. *Educational Accountability: Beyond Behavioral Objectives.* Washington, D.C.: Association for Supervision and Curriculum Development, 1972.

Nuffield Mathematics Project. *Checking Up.* New York: John Wiley & Sons, Inc., 1970.

Rance, Peter. *Record Keeping in the Progressive Primary School.* London: Ward Lock Educational Co., Ltd., 1971.

Tobier, Arthur, Ed. *Evaluation Reconsidered: A Position Paper and Supporting Documents on Evaluating Change and Changing Evaluation.* New York: Workshop Center for Open Education, May 1973.

CHAPTER 6. *A FOCUS ON GETTING STARTED*

Blitz, Barbara. *The Open Classroom: Making It Work.* Boston, Mass.: Allyn and Bacon, Inc., 1973.

Dennison, George. *The Lives of Children.* New York: Random House, Inc., 1969.

Hawkins, Frances P. *The Logic of Action.* Boulder, Colo.: University of Colorado, 1969.

Sargent, Betsye. *The Integrated Day in an American School.* Boston: National Association of Independent Schools, 1970.

Taylor, Joy. *Organizing the Open Classroom: A Teacher's Guide to the Integrated Day.* New York: Schocken Books, Inc., 1972.

Yeomans, Edward. *Schools Talk to Parents About the Integrated Day.* Boston: National Association of Independent Schools, 1971.

SPECIAL RESOURCES

Films

Children Are People (16 mm, color, 42 min.). Agathon Press Inc., 150 Fifth Avenue, New York, N.Y. 10011. A study of informal education in primary schools in England. Written and directed by Lorna Ridgway.

Children As People (16 mm, b/w, 35 min.). Polymorph Films, Inc., 331 Newbury St., Boston, Mass. 02115. John Holt narrates the film made at Fayerweather Street School in Cambridge. Children freely move about, talk, plan and direct their own work.

INFORMAL TEACHING IN THE OPEN CLASSROOM

Creative Spirit (16 mm, color, 25 min.). Available from National Audio-Visual Aids Library, Paxton Place, Gypsy Road, London, S.E. 27, England. English children on a field trip develop sketches, collect materials, and gain impetus for creative ideas that later result in finished projects after considerable work in the classroom. The experimental experience is shown as a basis for further inquiry and as a stimulus for creative learning.

Discovery and Experience (A series of 10 films—*Learning by Doing, Maths Is a Monster, Our Own Music, Learning by Design, Finding Out, Movement in Time and Space, The Changeover, City Infants, The Growing Mind, How Children Think*) 16 mm, b/w 30 min. Produced by British Broadcasting Corporation. Available in USA from Time-Life Films. These films illustrate the importance of activity, experience, and exploration for primary children. Filmed in various English Infant and Junior Schools, each focuses in on an area of learning to show informal teaching methods.

Eveline Lowe (16 mm, b/w, 30 min.). Available from Time-Life Films, Inc. A visit to a new open-plan school in London shows not only architectural features of working bays and a creative outside environment but also discusses the rationale for informal teaching.

I Am Here Today (16 mm, b/w, 43 min.). Educational Development Center, Inc., 39 Chapel Street, Newton, Mass. 02160. The integrated day approach in a classroom of 5-, 6-, 7-year-olds is shown. Filmed in Shady Hill School in Cambridge, Mass. Betsye Sargent is the teacher.

I Do and I Understand (16 mm, b/w, 14 min.). Available from Educational Foundation for Visual Aids, 33 Queen Anne Street, London WIM OAL (England). Made for the Nuffield Mathematics Teaching Project in 1964, this film is concerned with method. Nine-year-olds are shown in an activity-discovery approach to learning math.

Infants School (16 mm, b/w, 32 min.). Educational Development Center, Inc. Filmed at Gordonbrock Infant School in England by Lillian Weber, the scenes follow the children as they move in and out of two classrooms, a big hall, and outdoors. An active informal approach to learning is emphasized.

Learning About Thinking and Vice Versa (16 mm, b/w, 32 min.). Film Bureau, 267 West 25th Street, New York, N.Y. 10001. A film about how teachers can learn more about children's thinking. The action focuses on a workshop for teachers with teachers discussing their own teaching problems and classic Piaget interviews conducted by Eleanor Duckworth.

Living and Learning in the Open Classroom (16 mm, color, 29 min.). International Center for Educational Development, 16161 Ventura

Blvd., Encino, Calif. 91316. Filmed in several schools in Southern California, scenes show the open classroom at work. The teacher's role, children's planning, active learning, classroom environment, and a teachers' workshop are discussed and shown. Written and directed by Virgil Howes and others.

Maths Alive (16 mm, color, 30 min.). Available from Educational Foundations for Visual Aids. Primary school children are shown learning math from their own discoveries. Filmed in Great Britain by J. Howard for the Department of Education and Science and the Schools Council.

Open Classroom (16 mm, b/w, 12½ min.). Sherwin Rubin, 4532 Newton St., Torrance, Calif. 90505. A documentary filmed in a classroom in Southern California, the scenes introduce and explain an open classroom approach—one of structured freedom.

Primary Adventure (16 mm, color, 40 min.). Inner London Education Authority, The County Hall, London, SE1, England. A film about inner London's primary schools contrasting the schools of the later 1800's and those of the 1970's. Most of the film concentrates on informal teaching and purposeful activity of the children busily engaged in learning.

Prior Weston (16 mm, color, 15 min.). Center Office of Information, Hercules Road and Westminster Bridge Road, London S.E. 1, England. The headmaster, Henry Pluckrose, describes the change occurring in primary education in England today. A look at informal education in an urban London school is shown in a variety of scenes of children at work.

The Informal Classroom (16 mm, color, 15 min.). Educational Coordinates, 432 S. Pastoria Ave., Sunnyvale, Calif. 94086. Filmed in the Grape Street School in Watts, California, scenes show the open classroom at work in an inner-city school. Principal Carrie Haynes describes some of the goals and the focus of the program.

What Did You Learn at School Today? (16 mm, color, 43 min.). Leichestershire County Library, Clarence Street, Leichestershire LE13RW, England. A film about Leicestershire schools and their focus on the view that "the most valuable education is self-education, the best discipline self-discipline." It shows the importance of school environment, creativity, self-expression, and personal relationships.

What Is Teaching; What Is Learning? (16 mm, color, 30 min.). National Audio Visual Center, National Archives and Records Service, Washington, D.C. 20409. A film depicting what happens in a classroom while teachers responsible for what you see discuss the theory and philosophy behind what they are doing.

INFORMAL TEACHING IN THE OPEN CLASSROOM

Cassette Tapes

Available from Internaional Center for Educational Development, Encino, Calif.

Individualizing Teaching and Learning (six 1-hr tapes) by Virgil M. Howes and Robert E. Keuscher. Listener Corporation.

Individualized Reading (five 1-hr tapes) by Jeannette Veatch. Listener Corporation.

Involving the Child in Math (four 1-hr tapes) by Moira McKenzie. Listener Corporation.

Piaget in Childhood Education (four 1-hr tapes) by David Elkind. Listener Corporation.

220